W9-BXH-117

DATE DUE

DEMCO, INC. 38-2931

Canada

Other Books of Related Interest:

Opposing Viewpoints Series

America's Global Influence

Garbage and Recycling

Mexico

At Issue Series

Green Cities

Is Socialism Harmful?

Should the United States Be Multilingual?

Should There Be an International Climate Treaty?

Current Controversies Series

The Global Impact of Social Media

Illegal Immigration

The Uninsured

"Congress shall make no law . . . abridging the freedom of speech, or of the press."

First Amendment to the US Constitution

The basic foundation of our democracy is the First Amendment guarantee of freedom of expression. The *Opposing Viewpoints* series is dedicated to the concept of this basic freedom and the idea that it is more important to practice it than to enshrine it.

OPPOSING VIEWPOINTS® SERIES

Canada

Margaret Haerens, Book Editor

GREENHAVEN PRESS
A part of Gale, Cengage Learning

GALE
CENGAGE Learning™

Detroit • New York • San Francisco • New Haven, Conn • Waterville, Maine • London

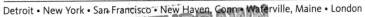

Christine Nasso, *Publisher*
Elizabeth Des Chenes, *Managing Editor*

© 2011 Greenhaven Press, a part of Gale, Cengage Learning

Gale and Greenhaven Press are registered trademarks used herein under license.

For more information, contact:
Greenhaven Press
27500 Drake Rd.
Farmington Hills, MI 48331-3535
Or you can visit our Internet site at gale.cengage.com

For product information and technology assistance, contact us at

Gale Customer Support, 1-800-877-4253
For permission to use material from this text or product, submit all requests online at www.cengage.com/permissions

Further permissions questions can be emailed to permissionrequest@cengage.com

Articles in Greenhaven Press anthologies are often edited for length to meet page require-ments. In addition, original titles of these works are changed to clearly present the main thesis and to explicitly indicate the author's opinion. Every effort is made to ensure that Greenhaven Press accurately reflects the original intent of the authors. Every effort has been made to trace the owners of copyrighted material.

Cover image copyright © Elena Elisseeva/Shutterstock.com.

LIBRARY OF CONGRESS CATALOGING-IN-PUBLICATION DATA

Canada / Margaret Haerens, book editor.
    p. cm. -- (Opposing viewpoints)
Includes bibliographical references and index.
ISBN 978-0-7377-5211-3 (hardcover) -- ISBN 978-0-7377-5212-0 (pbk.)
1. Canada--Social conditions--21st century. 2. Canada--Politics and government--21st century. 3. Canada--Environmental conditions. 4. Canada--Foreign relations--21st century. 5. Canada--Foreign relations--United States. 6. United States--Foreign relations--Canada. I. Haerens, Margaret.
    F1021.2.C364 2011
    971.07--dc22
                                                                    2010044206

Printed in the United States of America
1 2 3 4 5 6 7 15 14 13 12 11

Contents

Chapter 3: What Challenges to Freedom of Expression Does Canada Face?

Chapter 4: What Issues Are Impacting Canada–US Relations?

Why Consider Opposing Viewpoints?

> *"The only way in which a human being can make some approach to knowing the whole of a subject is by hearing what can be said about it by persons of every variety of opinion and studying all modes in which it can be looked at by every character of mind. No wise man ever acquired his wisdom in any mode but this."*
>
> *John Stuart Mill*

In our media-intensive culture it is not difficult to find differing opinions. Thousands of newspapers and magazines and dozens of radio and television talk shows resound with differing points of view. The difficulty lies in deciding which opinion to agree with and which "experts" seem the most credible. The more inundated we become with differing opinions and claims, the more essential it is to hone critical reading and thinking skills to evaluate these ideas. Opposing Viewpoints books address this problem directly by presenting stimulating debates that can be used to enhance and teach these skills. The varied opinions contained in each book examine many different aspects of a single issue. While examining these conveniently edited opposing views, readers can develop critical thinking skills such as the ability to compare and contrast authors' credibility, facts, argumentation styles, use of persuasive techniques, and other stylistic tools. In short, the Opposing Viewpoints Series is an ideal way to attain the higher-level thinking and reading skills so essential in a culture of diverse and contradictory opinions.

In addition to providing a tool for critical thinking, *Opposing Viewpoints* books challenge readers to question their own strongly held opinions and assumptions. Most people form their opinions on the basis of upbringing, peer pressure, and personal, cultural, or professional bias. By reading carefully balanced opposing views, readers must directly confront new ideas as well as the opinions of those with whom they disagree. This is not to argue simplistically that everyone who reads opposing views will—or should—change his or her opinion. Instead, the series enhances readers' understanding of their own views by encouraging confrontation with opposing ideas. Careful examination of others' views can lead to the readers' understanding of the logical inconsistencies in their own opinions, perspective on why they hold an opinion, and the consideration of the possibility that their opinion requires further evaluation.

Evaluating Other Opinions

To ensure that this type of examination occurs, *Opposing Viewpoints* books present all types of opinions. Prominent spokespeople on different sides of each issue as well as well-known professionals from many disciplines challenge the reader. An additional goal of the series is to provide a forum for other, less known, or even unpopular viewpoints. The opinion of an ordinary person who has had to make the decision to cut off life support from a terminally ill relative, for example, may be just as valuable and provide just as much insight as a medical ethicist's professional opinion. The editors have two additional purposes in including these less known views. One, the editors encourage readers to respect others' opinions—even when not enhanced by professional credibility. It is only by reading or listening to and objectively evaluating others' ideas that one can determine whether they are worthy of consideration. Two, the inclusion of such viewpoints encourages the important critical thinking skill of objectively evaluating an author's credentials and bias. This evaluation will illuminate an author's reasons for taking a particular stance on an issue and will aid in readers' evaluation of the author's ideas.

It is our hope that these books will give readers a deeper understanding of the issues debated and an appreciation of the complexity of even seemingly simple issues when good and honest people disagree. This awareness is particularly important in a democratic society such as ours in which people enter into public debate to determine the common good. Those with whom one disagrees should not be regarded as enemies but rather as people whose views deserve careful examination and may shed light on one's own.

Thomas Jefferson once said that "difference of opinion leads to inquiry, and inquiry to truth." Jefferson, a broadly educated man, argued that "if a nation expects to be ignorant and free . . . it expects what never was and never will be." As individuals and as a nation, it is imperative that we consider the opinions of others and examine them with skill and discernment. The *Opposing Viewpoints* series is intended to help readers achieve this goal.

David L. Bender and Bruno Leone,
Founders

Introduction

> *"Living next to you is in some ways like sleeping with an elephant. No matter how friendly and even-tempered is the beast, if I can call it that, one is affected by every twitch and grunt."*
>
> —Pierre Trudeau,
> *former Canadian prime minister*
> *during an address to the National*
> *Press Club in Washington, D.C., in 1969*

On paper the relationship between Canada and the United States is a close one. The two countries are the world's largest trading partners, exchanging an estimated $1.6 billion a day in goods. They share the world's longest unmilitarized border, which spans across 5,525 miles. More than three hundred thousand people cross that border every day. Politically, the two countries share common goals and work together on a number of issues, including geopolitical conflicts, North American security, environmental concerns, and economic matters. Culturally, Canada and the United States share similar values of tolerance and freedom as well as a common British heritage. Historians consider it one of the most successful international relationships in the modern world. It has been so valued for both countries that US and Canadian politicians have designated it "a special relationship" for many years.

In practice, however, that special relationship between Canada and the United States is often fraught with conflict over differing global policies and priorities. Like most close neighbors, times of disagreement and disappointment have occurred. Depending on the political leanings of the administration in power at any given time, the special relationship may be at the forefront of that nation's political priorities or not. Yet despite the tenor of the relationship at any given moment, both countries recognize the significance of the bond between them and have worked to maintain that bond. It has been essential to the security and economic success of both countries to ensure that the US-Canadian relationship remains strong and vibrant and continues to strengthen and evolve.

A long and storied history exists between the United States and Canada. It can be traced to the mid-sixteenth century, as English and French settlers and trappers moved back and forth over what would later become the border between the two countries. During the American Revolution, however, Canada remained loyal to England while America broke free and gained its independence.

Once the war ended in 1783, the British refused to abandon all of their military forts south of the Great Lakes border, which they had agreed to do. Tensions over the continued British presence and its interference in American affairs erupted into the War of 1812, when America declared war on Britain. The United States decided to invade Canada, hoping it would force Britain to negotiate and give up interest in American political affairs. American forces did succeed in invading and burning the Canadian city of York, now known as Toronto, on April 27, 1813. Most of the invasions failed, however, and a peace treaty took effect in February 1815. For the young nation of Canada, the hard-fought resistance to the American invasion during the War of 1812 was a defining moment.

The relationship between the United States and Canada was also strained during the American Civil War (1861–65), when Britain supported the Confederacy. Boundary disputes, especially in Alaska, also caused conflict between the two countries. Canada was enraged by the 1930 Smoot-Hawley Tariff Act, a US law that raised taxes on products imported from Canada. Canada responded with higher tariffs against

American products, and US-Canadian trade fell by 75 percent, further exacerbating the economic downturn for both countries during a time known as the Great Depression.

World War II (1939–45), however, ushered in a new era of friendship between Canada and the United States. The two nations cooperated closely on security during the war, recognized their mutual interests in protecting their western coasts from Japanese attacks, and coordinated a mutually beneficial strategy. Canada remained a close ally of the United States during the Cold War (1945–89), recognizing its growing importance on the world stage as one of the world's biggest superpowers. Canadian forces fought alongside Americans during the Korean (1950–53) and Gulf (1990–91) wars. Trade between the two countries grew, and they often worked together on a wide range of issues.

In recent years, Canada has remained a staunch ally of the United States in many ways. In 1987 the two countries signed the Canadian-American Free Trade Agreement, which eliminated the tariffs on most goods traded between them. Canadian forces have played an integral role in the war in Afghanistan, providing expert supervision and operational command capabilities.

In the past few years some new tensions have arisen. Canada's opposition to the US invasion of Iraq is one major example. There have been long-standing disputes over Canada's sovereignty over the Northwest Passage, a sea route through the Arctic Ocean that borders North America. Security issues have been another sticking point between the two countries: New passport requirements threaten trade and tourism and signal a change in the special relationship. Some Canadian political analysts derided the Stephen Harper administration for being too compliant to the George W. Bush administration and argued that the United States often took Canada for granted and overlooked its political and economic importance. Some conservative American political analysts excoriated Canada's opposition to the Iraq War, arguing that Canada should be fighting alongside them, like Britain and Australia.

Recognizing the growing tension, Canadian prime minister Stephen Harper began an effort to rehabilitate the bond between the two nations. "What has happened is that Canada lost that special relationship with the United States," he told an interviewer for *Maclean's* in December 2007. "We increasingly became viewed as just another foreign country, albeit an ally, a good friend, but nevertheless a foreign country. You know, the northern equivalent of Mexico in terms of the border. That isn't just a shift in the view of the administration, that's somewhat a shift in American public opinion as well, which concerns me."

In a speech in the House of Commons as Leader of the Opposition on May 28, 2002, Harper laid out his own view of the US-Canadian relationship. "Not only does the United States have this special relationship to us, it is the world leader when it comes to freedom and democracy," he maintained. "If the United States prospers, we prosper. If the United States hurts or is angry, we will be hurt. If it is ever broadly attacked, we will surely be destroyed."

For his part, American president Barack Obama is on board with the effort to strengthen ties between the two nations. In February 2009, he revived a tradition whereby a new US president made his first foreign trip to Canada, emphasizing the importance of the special friendship between the United States and Canada. "I love this country," Obama said in Ottawa during the visit. "We could not have a better friend and ally."

The authors of the viewpoints presented in *Opposing Viewpoints: Canada* explore many of the issues impacting the Canadian-US relationship as well as Canadian domestic and foreign policy matters in the following chapters: What Domestic Issues Are Affecting Canada? What Are the Major Foreign Policy Issues in Canada? What Challenges to Freedom of Expression Does Canada Face? and What Issues Are Impacting Canada–US Relations? The information in this volume will provide insight into the many challenges faced by Canada economically, environmentally, culturally, and politically in recent years.

OPPOSING VIEWPOINTS® SERIES

CHAPTER 1

What Domestic Issues Are Affecting Canada?

Chapter Preface

On July 22, 2010, the International Court of Justice ruled that Kosovo's secession from Serbia did not violate international law. Half a world away, this ruling by the international court gave renewed hope to a political movement hoping to break away from its mother country to establish its own independence: the Quebec sovereignty movement. The group advocates *sovereignty association* or *sovereignty partnership*, which means that Quebec would attain full independence from Canada, but would maintain a favored economic and political relationship with it.

For decades, the Quebec sovereignty movement has tried to muster political support for a greater level of independence from Canada. Members of the movement argue that Canada's federalist system as it stands does not respect Quebec's distinctive social, political, and economic position and fear that the English-Canadian majority will eventually water down Quebec's uniquely French-Canadian culture to the point where it will disappear. Of particular concern is the issue of language: Can a predominantly French-speaking people retain their language and culture surrounded by an English-Canadian majority?

Historically, Quebec has always shown an interest in a high level of self-determination and independence. The separatist movement began gathering momentum in the 1960s, when several political parties were formed with the stated goal to increase Quebec self-determination in political, cultural, and economic matters. The burgeoning movement caught international attention when French president Charles de Gaulle shouted "Vive le Québec libre!" during a speech from the balcony of Montreal's city hall in June 1967. A year later, the major pro-sovereignty groups united to form Parti Québécois (PQ). Their electoral successes in Quebec resulted in a 1977 law that made French the official language of the province and the 1980 Quebec referendum on sovereignty, which went down to defeat. A later referendum in 1995 was also closely defeated. Despite the popularity of the issue in Quebec political circles and amongst a huge segment of the people in the province, the issue of Quebec sovereignty has been put on the back burner in recent years, as other issues have taken precedence.

The International Court of Justice decision, however, has brought the issue back to the forefront. Supporters of Quebec sovereignty view the ruling as precedent for a possible future declaration of independence by the Quebec National Assembly. They take heart from the court's decision and hope to use it to reignite the fervor of sovereignty supporters and spur renewed calls for Quebec separatism. Opponents deride the ruling as not applicable to Quebec's enduring quest for self-determination and greater independence from Canada.

The question of whether Quebec sovereignty is still a viable and vibrant political and cultural movement is debated in the following chapter, which examines several of the major domestic issues affecting Canada. Other viewpoints in the chapter touch on the state of Canada's environment, the efficacy of the national health care system, and the impact of the global recession on the nation's economy.

> *"To ensure Canada's continued economic success while preserving these diverse ecosystems, governments should identify both the areas that can safely be used for economic activity as well as the areas that for ecological purposes should be left strictly undisturbed."*

Canada Has Made Much Environmental Progress

Kenneth P. Green and Ben Eisen

Kenneth P. Green is a resident scholar with the American Enterprise Institute for Public Policy Research and a member of the advisory board of the Frontier Centre for Public Policy. Ben Eisen is a policy analyst with the Frontier Centre for Public Policy. In the following viewpoint on the status of Canada's environment, they provide a hopeful assessment, maintaining that Canada's air, water, soil, and forests are adequately protected. Green and Eisen argue that the country is on the way to environmental sustainability.

Kenneth P. Green and Ben Eisen, "Executive Summary," *The Environmental State of Canada—30 Years of Progress*, FCPP Policy Series, No. 63, Frontier Centre for Public Policy, June 2009, pp. 5–8. Reprinted with permission.

As you read, consider the following questions:

1. According to the authors, how many people live in Canada?

2. By what percentage did GHG emissions per unit of economic productivity drop between 1990 and 2005 using inflation-adjusted dollars?

3. What percentage of cropland has been designated by the Canadian government as being at very low risk of wind erosion?

Canadians have much to celebrate concerning their natural environment. Over the past 30 years, Canada's air and water have become cleaner, ecosystems and timberlands have been preserved, and soils that feed not only Canadians but also many others around the world have been protected. This has happened while Canada's population and economy have grown strongly, which has propelled Canada, a country of only 33 million, to the status of an economic powerhouse with a standard of living that is the envy of much of the world. There is still more that can be done, but Canada is well on the way toward environmental sustainability.

Conventional Air Pollutants

The presence of a wide variety of pollutants influences air quality. No single indicator can be used as an adequate tool for analyzing overall air quality. For this reason, we examined the levels of four air pollutants in Canadian towns and cities that when taken together give a clear sense of the general trends in air quality.

- Of the four pollutants, two have dropped significantly in recent years, while two have remained virtually unchanged.

- Levels of sulphur dioxide and nitrogen dioxide are much lower in Canadian towns and cities than they were just a few decades ago. During the late 1970s, over 15 per cent of government monitoring stations reported concentrations of these pollutants that were above national air-quality objectives. By the early years of this decade [2000s], less than 1 per cent of stations reported unacceptable levels of nitrogen dioxide, and just 6 per cent recorded unacceptable concentrations of sulphur dioxide.

- For the third and fourth indicators, ground-level ozone and fine particulate matter, there has been neither a measurable drop nor a measurable increase since the early 1990s.

Due to these trends, a sizable majority of Canadian towns and cities now meet government-established quality standards for all four of these harmful pollutants. No community in Canada regularly exceeds quality standards for sulphur dioxide or nitrogen dioxide. Most communities that do not meet quality standards for fine particulate matter and ground-level ozone are concentrated in Ontario and Quebec. Across the rest of the country, almost all cities meet government air-quality standards for all four pollutants.

Greenhouse Gas (GHG) Emissions

The theory of human-induced global warming has provoked widespread concern in recent years. Due to the high level of interest in this issue, greenhouse gas [GHG] emissions, thought by many to contribute to global warming, has become the single most highly publicized indicator of environmental sustainability. Overall, Canada's performance using this indicator is perceived as unimpressive, particularly when compared with its peer countries. Whereas many industrialized countries have achieved significant reductions in their total GHG emissions since 1990, Canada's emissions have increased by over 20 per cent during this period.

However, despite vocal criticism from some environmental activists, trends in Canada's GHG emissions are not uniformly troubling. For example, our analysis of the GHG intensity indicator (GHG emissions per unit of GDP [gross domestic product]) suggests that Canada has made significant progress in this area when emissions per unit of economic activity are measured—a metric that is useful in a country where population and economic growth are the norm. Using inflation-adjusted dollars, GHG emissions per unit of economic productivity dropped 18 per cent between 1990 and 2005. Although some countries such as the United Kingdom have made even more impressive strides according to this indicator, the widespread perception that Canada has made no progress toward controlling its GHG emissions is mistaken.

Freshwater Withdrawals

Given its rich supply of freshwater and its comparatively small population, Canada withdraws a small percentage of its freshwater resources each year. While Canada's NAFTA [North American Free Trade Agreement] trading partners, the United States and Mexico, withdraw 17 per cent and 19 per cent respectively of their renewable freshwater each year, Canada withdraws just 1.6 per cent of its resources. These numbers suggest that Canada could safely withdraw several multiples more annually than it does now without straining its freshwater resources or having any measurable impact on their sustainability.

In the future, countries that have abundant freshwater will have the opportunity to help the water-poor countries of the world while promoting their own economic development through freshwater exports. Canadian governments should carefully oversee large-scale water exports to ensure that Canada's freshwater resources are not overused. While depletion of these resources should obviously not be permitted, the economic opportunities presented by Canada's renewable freshwater should not be wasted. The extent to which Canadians benefit from the country's natural endowment of freshwater would be significantly enhanced by policy changes that permit more water exports to Canada's NAFTA trading partners.

Although water is abundant in Canada, wasting such a valuable resource is undesirable. Canadians are among the heaviest users of water in the world. A major reason for this high level of water use is that many Canadians pay less than the market price for their water, and in many cases, they pay significantly less than the cost of water processing and delivery. This situation promotes waste and the inefficient use of water. By promoting arrangements in which the cost of water is driven by how much water consumers actually use, governments can improve the efficiency of water use, thereby creating circumstances under which Canada's freshwater resources will be put to the best possible use.

Freshwater Quality

Canada is blessed with abundant freshwater resources. The utility and value of freshwater, however, depends largely on its cleanliness. Due to the large number of factors that influence water quality, the federal government created a Water Quality Index [WQI] to obtain an overall picture of freshwater quality. Based on their WQI scores, all monitored freshwater sites are given a rating on a five-tiered scale that runs from poor on one end to excellent on the other.

This indicator suggests that water quality throughout Canada is quite good.

- More than twice as many monitored sites fell into one of the top two designations, good and excellent, than fell into one of the bottom two designations, marginal and poor.

- Canada's record in this area is also strong compared with its peer countries. According to the Environmental Protection Index, Canada has the second-highest level of water quality among G8 [Group of Eight, an intergovernmental organization comprising the world's leading industrialized nations] countries, behind only Italy.

Steps have been taken to further improve the quality of Canadian water in the years ahead, notably, dramatic improvements in the quality of wastewater treatment. In 1983, 28.3 per cent of sewers in Canada received no wastewater treatment.

By 1999, all but 3.4 per cent of sewers received some level of treatment. The percentage of sewers that received sophisticated secondary and tertiary treatments also grew during this period, from 55.8 per cent in the early 1980s to 77.7 per cent by the late 1990s. Wastewater discharges are a major source of water pollution, and the rapid improvement over recent years in the quality of wastewater treatment will help ensure that water pollution levels continue to remain low.

Soil Quality

A number of measurement tools have been developed to provide useful indicators of soil health. One such indicator is the Soil Organic Carbon Change Indicator which estimates changes in organic carbon levels in agricultural soil over time. According to this indicator, Canadian soil quality has improved dramatically in recent years. Whereas in the early 1980s, Canada experienced a significant annual net loss in soil organic carbon, by the early 2000s, Canada enjoyed large annual net gains.

This [viewpoint] examines the extent to which farmland is seen by the Government of Canada to be at risk of wind, soil, and tillage erosion. Canada has experienced a significant improvement according to these three indicators. The percentage

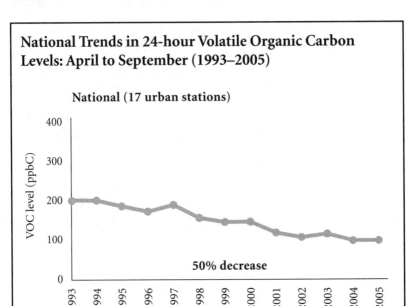

National Trends in 24-hour Volatile Organic Carbon Levels: April to September (1993–2005)

National (17 urban stations)

50% decrease

TAKEN FROM: Kenneth P. Green and Ben Essen, *The Environmental State of Canada*, FCPP, 2009. Government of Canada, *Five-Year Progress Report: Canada-wide Standards for Particulate Matter and Ozone*, 2007.

of cropland designated by the federal government as being at very low risk of wind erosion (the lowest possible designation) reached 86 per cent in 2001, up from 72 per cent in 1981, i.e., more land than ever is mostly safe from erosion. Similarly, the percentage of cropland deemed to be at very low risk of tillage erosion increased by over 30 per cent during this period.

Farm productivity, overall crop quality and variety, and total cash income from agriculture and agricultural exports have all risen in recent decades, partially due to the improvements in soil quality. This growth in farm productivity and the improvements in soil quality suggest that Canadian agricultural practices have become markedly more productive and sustainable over the course of the past 20 years.

Ecosystem Conservation

Canada contains a wide variety of ecosystems, each of which supports different types of animal and plant life. To ensure Canada's continued economic success while preserving these diverse ecosystems, governments should identify both the areas that can safely be used for economic activity as well as the areas that for ecological purposes should be left strictly undisturbed.

One primary tool governments can use to accomplish this is the ability to demarcate protected areas where large-scale commercial development is banned. In 1989, just 3 per cent of Canada's land area was protected by legislation. By 2003, that number rose to 8.4 per cent. Some provinces have been particularly aggressive in expanding their protected areas. Manitoba, British Columbia, and Nova Scotia are among the provinces that have significantly expanded their total protected land area since the late 1980s.

Forestry

The challenge facing governments in forest management is how to ensure Canadians maximize the opportunities for economic activity that are provided by the forests while also ensuring that the forests are sustainably managed. To achieve these objectives, Canadian governments regulate the amount of wood harvested each year. These regulations are generally specified as an Annual Allowable Cut (AAC). Ideally, actual annual forest harvests would be perfectly aligned with the AAC. For this reason, one indicator of success in forest management is the degree of alignment between the AAC and the actual quantity of harvested timber. Throughout the past decade, the actual timber harvest across Canada has been consistently significantly below the permitted AAC. This is especially true in the case of hardwood lumber. In 2006, the hardwood harvest was 35 million cubic metres, which is less than 60 per cent of that year's AAC, which was set at 60 million cubic metres. In the case of softwood lumber, harvests have consistently been approximately 20 per cent below the aggregate national AAC throughout the past 10 years—though it should be noted that there were other factors contributing to that lower level of harvesting including softwood lumber disputes with the United States and the mountain pine beetle epidemic.

Although this means the forest harvests have been sustainable, it also means opportunities for sustainable economic activity have been foregone even though they would not be environmentally problematic under current allowable cut levels. That Canada's forests are currently well managed is further attested to by a second indicator—trends in the total area of forest cover in Canada. Throughout the past decade, Canada's total forest cover has held steadily at approximately 310 million acres, 34 per cent of Canada's land mass.

"*Now there's a real danger that the oil sands project could join the seal hunt and the logging of old-growth forests as an emblem of this country's perceived environmental indifference.*"

Canada's Environmental Policies Have Led to Worldwide Criticism

Jonathon Gatehouse

Jonathan Gatehouse is a reporter for Maclean's, *Canada's national weekly current affairs magazine. In the following viewpoint, he outlines the worldwide concern over Canada's environmental policies, especially negotiations on a global agreement on curbing greenhouse gas emissions. Gatehouse points to the country's development of oil sands as a key reason Canada has gone from leader to laggard on the efforts to reduce greenhouse gases.*

As you read, consider the following questions:

1. What percentage of global greenhouse gas is Canada responsible for, according to the viewpoint?

Jonathon Gatehouse, "Suddenly the World Hates Canada," *Maclean's*, December 15, 2009. Reprinted with permission.

2. How did Stephen Harper's Conservative government change the country's obligations to the Kyoto Protocol?

3. According to Gatehouse, how much will greenhouse gas emissions from the oil sands increase between 2006 and 2020?

For decades, Canada has taken pride in punching above its weight on the international stage. Now it appears we're the ones absorbing the body blows. As scientists, activists, diplomats, and political leaders gather in Copenhagen [Denmark] for the United Nations' 15th convention on climate change, Dec. 7 to Dec. 18 [2009], the Northern Hemisphere's "helpful fixer" is undergoing a radical—and unrelentingly negative—image makeover. Canada "is now to climate what Japan is to whaling," George Monbiot, a columnist for the U.K.'s *Guardian* newspaper, thundered late last month, citing the [Stephen] Harper government's go-slow negotiating stance as "the major" obstacle to a new global agreement on curbing greenhouse gas emissions. "Until now I believed that the nation that has done the most to sabotage a new climate change agreement was the United States," wrote Monbiot, a green campaigner and best-selling author. "I was wrong. The real villain is Canada."

World Opinion and Canada

And he is not alone in that opinion. At a UN [United Nations] climate conference in Bangkok [Thailand] in October, delegates from developing countries walked out of a negotiating session (en masse, say environmental groups who were at the meeting; just five or six countries, counters Michael Martin, our ambassador for climate change) to protest Canada's suggestion that the Kyoto Protocol—the basis for the Copenhagen negotiations—be replaced with an entirely new anti-warming pact. In early November, at another UN meeting in Barcelona [Spain], Canada was named "Fossil of the Week" by the 450 nongovernmental organizations (NGOs) in attendance for its efforts to "block or stall" climate negotiations. ("If the price for having strong, capable, tough negotiators at the table is being singled out," Environment Minister Jim Prentice said at the time, "then so be it. Bring it on.")

During the Commonwealth summit in Trinidad and Tobago at the end of November, UN Secretary-General Ban Ki-moon pointedly called for Canada to pick up the pace of negotiations and adopt "ambitious" greenhouse gas reduction targets. And a coalition of scientists and NGOs asked the 53-nation body to suspend Canada's membership—a punishment that in the past has been meted out to such rogue states as Zimbabwe and apartheid-era South Africa—for "threatening the lives of millions of people in developing countries" through its inaction on climate change.

"Canada is effectively negotiating in bad faith, undermining the whole agreement," says Saleemul Huq, a lead author for the Intergovernmental Panel on Climate Change (IPCC) who joined in the suspension calls. "At least everyone else is trying to reach their Kyoto targets. Canada is doing absolutely nothing."

How Did Canada Become an Environmental Villain?

The question is how a country that is responsible for about two per cent of global greenhouse gas (GHG) emissions (China and the United States are collectively responsible for around 35 per cent) has come to take such a disproportionate share of the blame. The answer is a mixture of politics, bad timing, and—if Canada's critics are to believed—ill intentions.

When Jean Chrétien's Liberal government signed the Kyoto Protocol in April 1998, after years of international negotiations, there were significant doubts about whether the treaty would ever actually come into force. Although 187 countries are party to the deal, Kyoto only called for a few dozen developed nations to cut their emissions, and wasn't legally binding until countries representing 55 per cent of global carbon dioxide emissions as of 1990 gave it political ratification. (That occurred in December 2005 after the Russian Duma's surprise endorsement.) Even then, Canada's agreed target—a 6 per cent GHG reduction from 1990 levels by 2012—was based on another assumption: that the United States would at least try to move toward its own 8 per cent reduction target, even if Congress failed to ratify the deal. But George W. Bush beat Al Gore in the 2000 election, and the issue of global warming went into a political deep freeze in the U.S.

John Drexhage, one of Canada's Kyoto negotiators, now director of climate change and energy for the International Institute for Sustainable Development in Ottawa, says the sensible thing for the Liberals to do at that point was return to the table and ask for a break. Instead, Chrétien pushed ahead, having Parliament ratify the treaty in December 2002, burnishing his own legacy, and leaving it to his successor, Paul Martin, to try to figure out how to live up to the commitment. "The Liberals do deserve some share of the blame," says Drexhage. "It started with them trying to find loopholes—undermining the integrity of the treaty—rather than taking concrete action to reach our target."

A Change in Policy

When Stephen Harper's Conservatives took power in January 2006, they followed through on a campaign promise to flat out reject Canada's Kyoto obligations. Instead, the Tories have since pledged to reduce Canada's GHG emissions by 20 per cent from 2006 levels by 2020 (effectively half of what we promised under Kyoto, eight years later), leaving the details in limbo until the Americans flesh out their own climate change plans. The new target falls far short of the 25–40 per cent reduction from 1990 levels that scientists say industrialized countries must achieve by 2020, if the world is to limit warm-

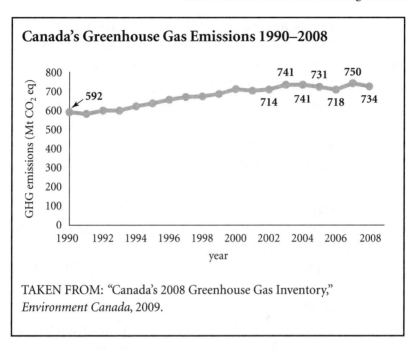

Canada's Greenhouse Gas Emissions 1990–2008

TAKEN FROM: "Canada's 2008 Greenhouse Gas Inventory,"
Environment Canada, 2009.

ing to just 2° C and avoid the most catastrophic effects of climate change. And many in the world community have expressed displeasure at Canada's modest goals. But what appears to have really put noses out of joint is the aggressive role this country has continued to play in the negotiations over Kyoto's next phase.

Time and again, Canada has seemed to find itself at odds with the international consensus around the negotiating table. At a Commonwealth meeting in Uganda in the fall of 2007, the Harper government blocked a resolution calling for a "binding commitment" on developed countries to reduce their emissions. (The prime minister said his government's view was that all nations, including emerging economic powerhouses like India, needed firm targets.) At the UN meetings in Poznan, Poland, in 2008, Canada spiked language about "aggregate targets" for the biggest emitters, as well as references to the UN Declaration on the Rights of Indigenous Peoples. In Bangkok in October the Canadian delegation insisted that

Kyoto-plus should also adopt 2006 as an optional base year—a change that would wipe out any obligation to deal with the country's 26 per cent rise in GHG emissions since 1990. In Barcelona, Canada quibbled over how climate change adaptation funds might be used—arguing they should not compensate nations for "loss and damage" due to impacts like rising sea levels. Now widely seen as a perpetual objector, Canada has become as welcome at climate conferences as a skunk at a garden party.

M.J. Mace, a climate negotiator for Micronesia [a subregion in Oceania] and the 37-member Alliance of Small Island States (AOSIS), is blunt when asked about her experiences with the Canadian delegation. "They're certainly polite, but in terms of substance, it's like they're thumbing their nose at the process," she says from Copenhagen. "And as we've gotten closer to putting numbers on the table, I think Canada has become more problematic." Mace describes the process of building a UN-style consensus on climate change as painstaking. But as everyone else struggles to move just from point A to point B, Canada frequently demands a detour to the margins of the map. "They have a lot of creative ideas that lead to circular discussions."

From Constructive to Obstructionist

The departure from Canada's traditional role as a bridge-builder at such international gatherings has not gone unnoticed. "Those who observe Canada's position and tactics definitely agree that we're not a constructive force," says Dale Marshall, a policy analyst with the David Suzuki Foundation's climate change program. "And Canada is an important enough player that you can't just gavel through things they object to." The finger-pointing and name-calling as Copenhagen gets under way are really just a public outpouring of frustrations that have been building for years behind closed doors. Marshall says that among NGOs, Canada's climate change reputation has been in the toilet for at least two years. "At the 2007 meeting in Bali, we tied the U.S. for 'fossil of the day' awards. But at every meeting since then, Canada has been the runaway winner. The 'Colossal Fossil.'"

Canada's Environment Minister Jim Prentice doesn't seem too rattled by the growing criticism of his government's record. In an interview shortly before he jetted off to Denmark, he said such concerns exist mostly in the Canadian media, not the minds of other players at the climate change summits. "I can tell you that we're at the table. We're constructive and we're active," said Prentice. "Not everyone always agrees with our positions, but we're there to put Canada's best interests forward, and we're doing that." Canada has been "forceful" in negotiations, but never obstructionist. "We've been quite outspoken in our view that the Kyoto Protocol is not working, but through it all we have been focused on achieving a new agreement," said Prentice, citing projections that 97 per cent of emissions growth in coming years will come from developing nations outside the original deal, like China and India.

Canada does recognize the need to reduce its own emissions rapidly, added the environment minister, but such significant economic changes can't be made overnight. "It's everything from the kind of cars we drive to how we produce electricity, to our consumption patterns and everything in between."

And for those who so clearly hope that the bad publicity will force Stephen Harper into a grand gesture at the summit, Prentice had a message: don't hold your breath. Canada's targets are firm, said Prentice, and the details of its climate change plan will be made public at the appropriate time—when it is clear what steps our NAFTA [North American Free Trade Agreement] partners will take—and at home, rather than some global forum. "I know there's angst about Canada's role, but Canada is not the issue at the Copenhagen negotiations. It's about bridging the gap between the developed and the developing world and arriving at a treaty that the Americans and the Chinese will sign."

Canada Is Falling Behind

But if such a deal—either a political framework, or less likely a binding treaty—does emerge in Denmark, will Canada find itself on the wrong side of the table? Earlier this fall, a Pew Center on Global Climate Change report ranking the commitments of developed countries lumped Canada in among the laggards. Japan has pledged to cut its emission 25 per cent below 1990 levels by 2020; Russia has done the same. The European Union target is 20 to 30 per cent. Even the current U.S. promises—a 17 per cent cut from 2005 levels by 2020—look to be more profound than what we have promised so far, especially once other U.S. measures like new fuel efficiency standards for cars and green energy initiatives are taken into account, which add up to a 28 to 34 per cent GHG reduction, according to another Washington think tank. (The U.S. is also promising an 83 per cent cut by 2050; Canada's target is "60 to 70" per cent of 2006 levels by the same year.) And the signs heading into the summit are that the developing world is also getting on board. The Brazilian government has indicated that it will be bringing proposals for reductions of 38 to 42 per cent of current levels by 2020 to Copenhagen. China has announced a goal of cutting the intensity of its carbon emissions 40 to 45 per cent by 2020, from 2005 levels. (It's a target that would mean slower emissions growth, but could see Chinese GHG output double.) India has embraced an intensity reduction of 20 to 25 percent by 2020 (which still might result in a 90 to 95 per cent increase in carbon emissions).

Miguel Lovera, a member of Paraguay's negotiating team in Copenhagen, says he has been puzzled by Canada's positions over the last few years. "We would have expected a much more compassionate role from them in solving this global problem." Canada, he notes, is among the world's top 10 GHG emitters in total (eighth), per capita (eighth), and cumulatively over the past century-and-a-half (10th). Lovera says Canada's negotiating positions—like using 2006 rather than 1990 as the base year—seem to be motivated by a desire to protect Alberta's oil sands development, rather than the planet. "How come the rest of the world is trying to reduce emissions, especially in fossil fuel production, and Canada has these plans to drastically expand the tar sands?" he asks. "That's really difficult to grasp." (Paraguay's GHG targets coming into Copenhagen are a 49 per cent reduction from 1990 levels by 2017, and a 95 per cent reduction by 2050.)

The Role of Oil Sands

In fact, for all the lip service about Canada's cold climate, vast distances and energy intensive industries, the reality is that going forward with the oil sands will be one of our biggest problems. A 2008 Environment Canada report estimated that GHG emissions from the oil sands will triple between 2006 and 2020, making it "the largest single contributor to Canada's medium-term emissions growth." That would make one energy project in one province responsible for 95 per cent of the country's projected increase in industrial emissions over that period. In other words, whatever brownie points Canada wins internationally for Quebec's pledge to reduce its GHG output by 20 per cent of 1990 levels by 2020 (the most ambitious target in North America) is nullified by Alberta's goal of simply stabilizing emissions by 2020; a 58 per cent increase from 1990 levels.

Canada argues, quite rightly, that the oil sands have become an engine of economic prosperity for the entire country, and a vital source of secure energy in a precarious world. But the government's aggressive efforts to protect our national interests, at perhaps the expense of global progress on climate change, haven't won us a lot of sympathy. Earlier this fall, Rajendra Pachauri, the head of the IPCC, suggested that Canada take a time-out on the oil sands, until carbon capture and storage techniques catch up to rapidly escalating emissions. And international campaigns against Alberta's "dirty oil" are picking up steam. Now there's a real danger that the oil sands project could join the seal hunt and the logging of old-growth forests as an emblem of this country's perceived environmental indifference.

"Canada is going to have to square the circle on what they are doing in the oil sands," says Melinda Kimble, a U.S. climate change negotiator during the [former president Bill] Clinton years, now senior vice president of the United Nations Foundation, a charity that backs the world body's initiatives. "Everyone at the table has national interests." Kimble says the disconnect between Canada's role in the Kyoto talks—"a very vital and constructive voice"—and its behaviour now is all the more surprising given the turnabout in the U.S. thinking on climate change since Barack Obama took office. (As the summit opened in Copenhagen, the U.S. Environmental Protection Agency followed through on the president's pledge to declare greenhouse gases a danger to public health, paving the way for strict new emissions regulations.) The Harper government has frequently said it intends to follow the U.S. lead on climate change, but now that the direction is clear, is it necessary to wait for Congress to hammer out all the details? "I'm sure the Bush administration was very glad to see countries like Canada and Australia acting in solidarity with the U.S.," says Kimble. "But there has been a leadership shift. I think Obama is determined to put in place greenhouse gas regulations."

Feeling the International Cold Shoulder

There have been suggestions that Canada is already feeling the cold shoulder because of its climate change foot-dragging. Ottawa certainly appeared taken aback by Obama's announcement that he will attend Copenhagen. (Prime Minister Harper followed suit and announced his own trip a couple of days later.) At the Commonwealth meeting there were suggestions that Canada was "sandbagged" by a joint French-British announcement of a $10-billion climate change adaptation fund. UN watchers say Canada's push for a rotational seat on the [UN] Security Council has been damaged, if not submarined, by climate concerns. And foreign diplomats in Ottawa have grown so frustrated that they have taken to calling NGOs to seek advice on how to get the Harper government's attention on the environment file.

Jeremy Kinsman, a retired diplomat who served as Canada's ambassador or high commissioner to 15 countries, including Russia and the United Kingdom, wonders why the government is bothering to stake out such a contentious position. "Canadians are acting as if we're terribly important to the Copenhagen summit." The reality, he says, is that "we're going to have to accept whatever comes out of this. We're going to have to go along with whatever the U.S. agrees." Canada is vulnerable, especially on the oil sands, both in terms of its international image and the looming climate change treaty. (Less generous credits for carbon sinks like our boreal forest would make Canada's reduction targets even more difficult to achieve.)

Kinsman sees a disturbing trend, where a government with a "disdain" for diplomacy has undercut Canada's traditional international role. "There's a general impression that Canada is not very engaged in the world anymore, except in Afghanistan," he says. But even then, from a seasoned diplomat's perspective, there is never an excuse for the way Canada has been acting at the climate change table. "In the end, it's not your position, it's how you behave," says Kinsman. "Influence is an asset and we've run it down."

"While the United States fears a prolonged recession, Canadians have remained relatively sanguine, convinced that they are in a good position to weather the economic tsunami from the south."

Canada's Economy Has Not Been Hard-Hit by the Global Economic Recession

Keith B. Richburg

Keith B. Richburg is a staff writer for the Washington Post. *In the following viewpoint, he reports that Canada has remained relatively insulated from the global financial crisis because of its more tightly regulated banking system. Richburg maintains that fears about the economy helped incumbent prime minister Stephen Harper and the Conservative Party in the 2008 elections.*

As you read, consider the following questions:

1. What does Richburg see as the main reason for optimism related to the Canadian economy?

Keith B. Richburg, "Worldwide Financial Crisis Largely Bypasses Canada," *Washington Post*, October 16, 2008. Reprinted with permission.

2. According to the Canadian Bankers Association, what is one reason for the banking system's solidity?

3. How has the US housing market slowdown affected Canada?

While the United States reels from the global financial crisis, with credit markets still frozen and stock prices careening from highs to lows, Canada has remained relatively insulated.

Canadian banks have not gone shaky like their American counterparts, economists and other experts said. There is no subprime mortgage or home foreclosure mess. And while the United States fears a prolonged recession, Canadians have remained relatively sanguine, convinced that they are in a good position to weather the economic tsunami from the south.

"We will be pulled down," said Michael Gregory, chief economist at BMO Nesbitt Burns, an investment firm. "Not as deep, not as long."

More Regulation Made the Difference

The main reason for optimism here is the banking system. Experts here note that Canadian banks are more tightly regulated, more liquid and less highly leveraged. Instead of being high-flying investment banks, they tend to operate in a more traditional manner, with large numbers of loyal depositors and a more solid base of capital.

"I think the regulatory framework in Canada is a little more stringent," Gregory said, "and Canadian banks are a little more conservative in terms of lending." The World Economic Forum this month [October 2008] rated Canada's banks as the world's soundest, ahead of banks in Sweden and Luxembourg.

According to the Canadian Bankers Association, one reason for the system's solidity is that banks are national in scope. Each of the largest five institutions has branches in all 10 Canadian provinces, meaning they are less susceptible to regional downturns and they can move capital from region to region, as needed. "As far as I am aware, no American bank has branches in all 50 states," banking association spokesman Andrew Addison wrote in an e-mail.

Mortgage Lending Is Also Strictly Regulated

Strict rules also govern mortgage lending. By Canadian law, any mortgage that will finance more than 80 percent of the price of a home must be insured. Two-thirds of all Canadian mortgages are insured by the quasi-governmental Canadian Mortgage and Housing Corp. As a result of the tough standards for insurance, "people tend not to get mortgages they cannot afford," Gregory said.

Defaulting on a loan is also more difficult in Canada than the United States, Gregory said. "You can't just drop off the keys and walk away."

For Canada's seven biggest banks, the percentage of mortgages at least three months in arrears was 0.27 percent in July [2008], close to historic lows, according to the banking association. Also, few Canadian banks got caught holding large numbers of toxic American mortgages.

Housing Market Is Tight

Another difference is that in Canada, mortgage interest is not tax-deductible, making it harder to buy a house. As a result, Canada did not have as strong a construction surge as the United States did during the boom years, and thus does not now have a big oversupply.

People do not take out mortgages just for the tax break. In Canada, "a mortgage is seen as something you want to get rid of as fast as possible," said Peter Dungan, an economist with the Rotman School of Management at the University of Toronto.

Amid this relative health, there have been reports that American companies, needing cash and credit, have been turning to their Canadian subsidiaries for short-term loans.

But Canada's economy has not been entirely trouble-free. The Toronto Stock Exchange is down. The appreciation of the Canadian dollar has harmed exports. The slowdown in the United States—which takes 80 percent of Canada's exports—has a direct impact here. In particular, the American housing troubles have hurt because much of the wood in new U.S. houses comes from Canada.

"What Americans are not buying is directly what we export," Dungan said.

Fears about the global crisis helped Prime Minister Stephen Harper increase his Conservative Party's presence in Parliament in Tuesday's elections [October 14, 2008], many analysts here believe, though the party still fell short of an absolute majority.

Harper called the election in September, just before the crisis hit. After some initial verbal stumbles—he at first seemed to play down the fall of the Toronto exchange—he campaigned as the steady hand to see Canada through hard economic times ahead.

Polls showed that the economy was the main issue in the election.

"The government's claims are so out-landish that even big mouthpieces of capitalism have taken their distance."

Canada's Economy Is Suffering from the Global Economic Recession

Roger Annis

Roger Annis is co-editor of the Socialist Voice *and a frequent contributor at the Global Research website. In the following viewpoint, he asserts that Canada's working class has been hard-hit by the global economic crisis. Annis criticizes the current government and the media for ignoring the effects of the recession on Canadians.*

As you read, consider the following questions:

1. According to Annis, what percentage of the net worth have Canadian households lost since June 2008?

2. What do bank analysts predict as Canada's budget deficit in fiscal 2009?

Roger Annis, "Economic Crisis Slams Canada," GlobalResearch.ca, March 29, 2009. www.globalresearch.ca. Reprinted with permission.

3. How do Canada's January–February 2009 job losses relate to the United States' job losses during the same period?

As the grim news of growing job losses mounts in Canada, the federal Conservative government is continuing the politics of denial that marked last autumn's election campaign [2008]. Especially troubling for the working class is that opposition political parties, including the trade union–based New Democratic Party, are offering no substantial alternative.

Economic Collapse by the Numbers

The first two months of 2009 were a disaster for working people; 240,000 workers lost their jobs. The job losses in January were the largest monthly loss ever in Canada. November to February losses are the steepest since the crushing recession of 1981/82.

Since June of 2008, Canadian households have lost 8% of their net worth. Household credit debt grew by 2% in the fourth quarter of 2008.

Two of the big three U.S. automakers in Canada, General Motors [GM] and Chrysler, say they will pack up operations in Canada if they don't receive nearly $10 billion of taxpayer bailout money. Together they employ some 20,000 workers in vehicle assembly and tens of thousands more in parts manufacture, sales, and service. Chrysler wants its workforce to concede even deeper cuts in wages and benefits than those voted by GM Canada workers in mid-March.

Cuts to social services will soon be the order of the day as governments cry poverty and deficits mount. Bank analysts say the federal government will have a budget deficit of $40 billion in fiscal 2009. The government of Ontario, the province with the largest manufacturing employment, has announced the largest budget deficit in the province's history for 2009, $14.2 billion.

If deep cuts to social services have not already begun, it's because the federal government and some provincial governments, notably in British Columbia, are positioning themselves for re-election before swinging their axes.

The Social Wage Threatened

Among the first victims of the economic downturn have been laid-off workers trying to collect unemployment insurance, and workers who are retired or soon to be.

Laid-off workers receive fewer benefits for shorter periods of time as a result of drastic cuts to the federal unemployment insurance program over the past years. According to Winnie Ng of the Good Jobs for All Coalition in Toronto, only 31% of unemployed workers receive benefits. Under pressure, the federal government recently extended by five weeks the length of time that recipients can collect. It did nothing to improve access.

Workers with retirement savings connected to the stock market have suffered double-digit losses in the past six months. Meanwhile, company pension plans at many of Canada's largest employers no longer have enough funds to pay established benefits, in part because companies have unilaterally cut their contributions in recent years. The highly profitable Canadian Pacific Railway, for example, allowed its pension deficit to triple in 2008, to $1.6 billion. Air Canada's deficit rose 172% that same year. GM Canada's shortfall is somewhere around $6 billion. Only 50% of GM's unionized workers' present and future benefits are covered.

The federal government is considering legislation that would extend to ten years, from the current five, the time allowed companies to make up pension plan shortfalls.

The public pension picture, once thought impervious to the vagaries of the stock market, is starting to look grim. The

© 2009 Graeme McKay. Reproduced with permission.

manager of public pension plans in the province of Quebec announced in February an astounding loss of nearly $40 billion in 2008, one-quarter of the value of its holdings, due to substantial investment in the stock market, including the riskiest of assets.

Losses in Canada's public plan, which covers residents of all provinces and territories except Quebec, were $18 billion, or 14% of value. A big part of the losses can be traced back to a decision by the federal government in 1999 to allow the plan to invest 25% of its assets in the stock market. One can only guess what the size of the 2008 loss would have been without that 25% cap.

What Economic Collapse?

In the face of the grim economic news, the message from the federal government is, "Don't worry, be happy." Prime Minister Stephen Harper told a business audience in Brampton, Ontario, on March 10 [2009]: "Canada was the last advanced country to fall into this recession. We will make sure its effects here are the least severe, and we will come out of this faster than anyone and stronger than ever."

The latest message from Harper repeats the denials he issued when the world financial collapse escalated in September 2008, coinciding with the beginning of the last federal election. As the financial decline broke over Canada that month, Harper famously declared that it would be a good time to invest in the stock market. By November, Canada's largest stock index had declined 44%. In March 2009, it still stands 39% lower.

The government's claims are so outlandish that even big mouthpieces of capitalism have taken their distance. No less than the International Monetary Fund, itself an agency promoting rosy prospects for a quick international economic recovery, said on March 17 that Canada's economy would shrink by 2% in 2009, double an earlier "estimate" of 1%.

Former Bank of Canada governor David Dodge says that Harper's claim that Canada will experience a quick recovery and lead the rest of the world out of its decline is "totally unrealistic."

Comparing Economies of the United States and Canada

Canada's media has been focused on the disastrous decline of the U.S. economy. But Canada's January/February 2009 job losses are higher by 50% on a per capita basis than the U.S., wrote *Vancouver Sun* columnist Barbara Yaffe on March 20.

She also pointed to another ominous comparison between the two economies. Canada's is far more dependent on exports than its U.S. counterpart. They account for 35% to 40% of Canada's gross domestic product, compared to 12% to 15% in the U.S. More than three-quarters of Canadian exports go to the ailing U.S.

Harper's Pollyanna-like message is echoed by the opposition parties in Parliament, all of whom followed the government's lead in downplaying the gravity of the economic collapse. Only now are they hinting at taking their distance.

Deputy NDP [New Democratic Party] Leader Thomas Mulcair expressed unease with the government's projections during a CBC Radio [broadcast] on March 24. "I'd like to have a clear-eyed view of what's really happening in the economy," he complained.

When asked what should be done for the country's unemployment insurance program, Mulcair said that the two-week waiting period should be eliminated. He decried the reduction in accessibility to the program but offered no measure to redress this.

The NDP announced on March 22 that it is launching a nine-week public consultation process to "investigate the effects of the recession on ordinary Canadians, and bring new ideas to Ottawa."

Subprime Mortgage Elephant in the Room

The March 14 *Globe and Mail* reported on a subject that no political party has dared to talk about, namely the troubling state of housing mortgages in Canada. Headlined "Canada's dirty subprime secret," the article began: "A *Globe and Mail* investigation into more than 10,000 foreclosure proceedings has uncovered a burgeoning subprime mortgage problem that many, including Prime Minister Stephen Harper, have insisted does not exist in Canada."

The federal government opened up Canada's mortgage market in early 2006 to reckless and predatory practices similar to those in the U.S. For example, 40-year mortgage amortization terms became legal for the first time, extended from 25 years. Requirements for down payments were also sharply lowered for the first time in history.

The *Globe* article reports that in Canada, statistics on housing loans are veiled in institutional secrecy. The full extent of consumer exposure to predatory lending cannot yet be assessed. The authors write, "The spread of subprime mortgages to Canada is one of the country's most poorly researched and misunderstood economic afflictions."

Where the authors could find statistics—on home foreclosures in the provinces of Alberta and British Columbia—they found fully half of them last year were on subprime loans. Foreclosures in both Alberta and British Columbia in 2008 were more than double the previous year. What is striking about those figures is that the two provinces experienced a resource-price economic boom until late in the year.

It's not only the ability to pay, or not, that has mortgage holders threatened with losing their homes. Lenders have lost the will, or ability, to lend. As a March 27 [2009] *Globe and Mail* report revealed, an estimated $3 billion to $5 billion in high-risk mortgages are up for renewal in the next four years and the original lenders do not have the necessary access to capital to renew them. They want the federal government to step in and provide the financing. As many as 25,000 mortgage holders are involved.

Profitable Banks?

From the capitalist standpoint, the one rosy picture in the Canadian economy is the performance of the country's highly monopolized banks. They all reported profits in the last quarter of 2008.

Government propaganda says that the banks in Canada are solid and not suffering from the same mistakes as their U.S. cousins. But that didn't prevent the government from quietly changing a law last November [2008] that would now permit it to purchase bank shares. Just in case. . . .

The previous month, the government authorized the purchase of up to $25 billion in bad loans and securities from the banks. That was boosted to $125 billion early in 2009.

The banks lost hundreds of millions of dollars from the stock market decline in 2008. Losses will deepen in 2009 as they are hit by the manufacturing downturn, declining profit rates, and the full onslaught of foreclosures and personal bankruptcies.

The financial liberalization of recent years has simply postponed a practice that is endemic to capitalism—producing more goods and services than can be sold for a profit. In countries like the United States and Canada, government borrowing abroad, easy consumer credit and all manner of financial fraud made it possible to postpone the contradiction between growing supply of goods and services, on the one hand, and exploitation-restricted demand, on the other.

They Must Pay for Their Folly, Not Us

Government bailouts of the financial industry are nothing but a massive transfer of wealth from the poor to the rich in order to prop up the very institutions and wealthy families that have brought economic calamity to the world in the first place.

"Stimulus" spending by capitalist governments is proving to be a similar boondoggle. The Canadian government announced a spending package in January [2009] to the tune of $40 billion. Some of it is earmarked for road and bridge repair, in other words to line the pockets of the very transportation designers and companies that have created urban transportation gridlock and brought the world to the precipice of irreversible climate catastrophe.

But where much of the spending will be targeted is completely unknown. Passage of enabling legislation is delayed because opposition parties are uneasy with a near-total lack of details of where the money will be spent and how it will be accounted for.

One thing that is known—the government has already said it will ease the process of environmental review of "stimulus" projects.

By far the most effective forms of "stimulus" spending would be to expand social services, including health care, education and child care; raise the salaries or welfare and pension benefits of the lowest paid in society; build public housing on a large scale; and undertake a massive program to redress the social and economic calamity lived by most of Canada's 1.8 million indigenous peoples.

This kind of spending would deliver immediate aid to hard-pressed individuals and families. It would reverse the damaging cuts to social services by governments in recent decades. It would also inject money directly into local economies.

A serious fight by trade unions and other social organizations for such "social stimulus" would strengthen the entire working-class movement and place it in a better position to wage struggles around a particularly vexing challenge—how to confront the jobs crisis in manufacturing industries.

A fight for an "ecological stimulus" is equally pressing. How can environmentally destructive industries such as automobile assembly, energy production, forestry and many others be transformed to produce socially useful products that do not trash the natural environment?

And how can a plan for a new economy take control out of the hands of corporations driven by greed and profit?

> "Like it or not . . . , publicly funded, universally available health care is simply the most powerful contributing factor to the overall health of the people who live in any country."

Canada's Health Care Is a Good System

Holly Dressel

Holly Dressel is a researcher and writer. In the following viewpoint, she maintains that the US system of privately funded health care has left the general health of the US population in worse shape than that of most industrialized countries, particularly Canada.

As you read, consider the following questions:

1. How many of the family bankruptcies filed every year in the United States are directly related to medical expenses, according to Dressel?

2. According to the author, when did US and Canadian health care results begin to diverge?

Holly Dressel, "Has Canada Got the Cure?" *Yes! Magazine*, August 4, 2006. Reprinted with permission.

3. What are the United States and Canada ranked on the US government ranking of infant mortality in 225 countries?

Should the United States implement a more inclusive, publicly funded health care system? That's a big debate throughout the country. But even as it rages, most Americans are unaware that the United States is the only country in the developed world that doesn't already have a fundamentally public—that is, tax-supported—health care system.

That means that the United States has been the unwitting control subject in a 30-year, worldwide experiment comparing the merits of private versus public health care funding. For the people living in the United States, the results of this experiment with privately funded health care have been grim. The United States now has the most expensive health care system on earth and, despite remarkable technology, the general health of the U.S. population is lower than in most industrialized countries. Worse, Americans' mortality rates—both general and infant—are shockingly high.

Different Paths

Beginning in the 1930s, both the Americans and the Canadians tried to alleviate health care gaps by increasing use of employment-based insurance plans. Both countries encouraged nonprofit private insurance plans like Blue Cross, as well as for-profit insurance plans. The difference between the United States and Canada is that Americans are still doing this, ignoring decades of international statistics that show that this type of funding inevitably leads to poorer public health.

Meanwhile, according to author Terry Boychuk, the rest of the industrialized world, including many developing countries like Mexico, Korea, and India, viscerally understood that "private insurance would [never be able to] cover all necessary hospital procedures and services; and that even minimal protection [is] beyond the reach of the poor, the working poor, and those with the most serious health problems." Today, over half the family bankruptcies filed every year in the United States are directly related to medical expenses, and a recent study shows that 75 percent of those are filed by people with health insurance.

The United States spends far more per capita on health care than any comparable country. In fact, the gap is so enormous that a recent University of California, San Francisco, study estimates that the United States would save over $161 billion every year in paperwork alone if it switched to a single-payer system like Canada's. These billions of dollars are not abstract amounts deducted from government budgets; they come directly out of the pockets of people who are sick.

The year 2000 marked the beginning of a crucial period, when international trade rules, economic theory, and political action had begun to fully reflect the belief in the superiority of private, as opposed to public, management, especially in the United States. By that year the U.S. health care system had undergone what has been called "the health management organization revolution." U.S. government figures show that medical care costs have spiked since 2000, with total spending on prescriptions nearly doubling.

Cutting Costs, Cutting Care

There are two criteria used to judge a country's health care system: the overall success of creating and sustaining health in the population, and the ability to control costs while doing so. One recent study published in the *Canadian Medical Association Journal* compares mortality rates in private for-profit and nonprofit hospitals in the United States. Research of 38 million adult patients in 26,000 U.S. hospitals revealed that death rates in for-profit hospitals are significantly higher than in nonprofit hospitals: for-profit patients have a 2 percent higher chance of dying in the hospital or within 30 days of discharge.

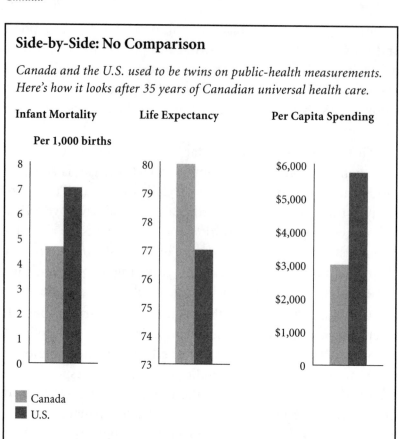

Side-by-Side: No Comparison

Canada and the U.S. used to be twins on public-health measurements. Here's how it looks after 35 years of Canadian universal health care.

Infant Mortality   **Life Expectancy**   **Per Capita Spending**

Per 1,000 births

Canada
U.S.

TAKEN FROM: World Health Organization, CIA, World Fact Book, Centers for Disease Control/Holly Dressel, "Has Canada Got the Cure?" *Yes! Magazine*, August 4, 2006.

The increased death rates were clearly linked to "the corners that for-profit hospitals must cut in order to achieve a profit margin for investors, as well as to pay high salaries for administrators."

"To ease cost pressures, administrators tend to hire less highly skilled personnel, including doctors, nurses, and pharmacists ...," wrote P.J. Devereaux, a cardiologist at McMaster University and the lead researcher. "The U.S. statistics clearly show that when the need for profits drives hospital decision making, more patients die."

The Value of Care for All

Historically, one of the cruelest aspects of unequal income distribution is that poor people not only experience material want all their lives, they also suffer more illness and die younger. But in Canada there is no association between income inequality and mortality rates—none whatsoever.

In a massive study undertaken by Statistics Canada in the early 1990s, income and mortality census data were analyzed from all Canadian provinces and all U.S. states, as well as 53 Canadian and 282 American metropolitan areas. The study concluded that "the relationship between income inequality and mortality is not universal, but instead depends on social and political characteristics specific to place." In other words, government health policies have an effect.

"Income inequality is strongly associated with mortality in the United States and in North America as a whole," the study found, "but there is no relation within Canada at either the province or metropolitan area level—between income inequality and mortality."

The same study revealed that among the poorest people in the United States, even a one percent increase in income resulted in a mortality decline of nearly 22 out of 100,000.

What makes this study so interesting is that Canada used to have statistics that mirrored those in the United States. In 1970, U.S. and Canadian mortality rates calculated along income lines were virtually identical. But 1970 also marked the introduction of Medicare in Canada—universal, single-payer coverage. The simple explanation for how Canadians have all become equally healthy, regardless of income, most likely lies in the fact that they have a publicly funded, single-payer health system and the control group, the United States, does not.

Infant Mortality

Infant mortality rates, which reflect the health of the mother and her access to prenatal and postnatal care, are considered one of the most reliable measures of the general health of a population. Today, U.S. government statistics rank Canada's infant mortality rate of 4.7 per thousand—23rd out of 225 countries, in the company of the Netherlands, Luxembourg, Australia, and Denmark. The U.S. is 43rd—in the company of Croatia and Lithuania, below Taiwan and Cuba.

All the countries surrounding Canada or above it in the rankings have tax-supported health care systems. The countries surrounding the United States and below have mixed systems or are, in general, extremely poor in comparison to the United States and the other G8 [Group of 8, an intergovernmental organization comprising the world's leading industrialized nations] industrial powerhouses.

There are no major industrialized countries near the United States in the rankings. The closest is Italy, at 5.83 infants dying per thousand, but it is still ranked five places higher.

In the United States, infant mortality rates are 7.1 per 1,000, the highest in the industrialized world—much higher than some of the poorer states in India, for example, which have public health systems in place, at least for mothers and infants. Among the inner-city poor in the United States, more than 8 percent of mothers receive no prenatal care at all before giving birth.

Overall U.S. Mortality

We would have expected to see steady decreases in deaths per thousand in the mid-twentieth century, because so many new drugs and procedures were becoming available. But neither the Canadian nor the American mortality rate declined much; in fact, Canada's leveled off for an entire decade, throughout the 1960s. This was a period in which private care was increasing in Canadian hospitals, and the steady mortality rates reflect the fact that most people simply couldn't afford the new therapies that were being offered. However, beginning in

1971, the same year that Canada's Medicare was fully applied, official statistics show that death rates suddenly plummeted, maintaining a steep decline to their present rate.

In the United States, during the same period, overall mortality rates also dropped, reflecting medical advances. But they did not drop nearly so precipitously as those in Canada after 1971. But given that the United States is the richest country on earth, today's overall mortality rates are shockingly high, at 8.4 per thousand, compared to Canada's 6.5.

Rich and Poor

It has become increasingly apparent, as data accumulate, that the overall improvement in health in a society with tax-supported health care translates to better health even for the rich, the group assumed to be the main beneficiaries of the American-style private system. If we look just at the 5.7 deaths per thousand among presumably richer, white babies in the United States, Canada still does better at 4.7, even though the Canadian figure includes all ethnic groups and all income levels. Perhaps a one-per-thousand difference doesn't sound like much. But when measuring mortality, it's huge. If the U.S. infant morality rate were the same as Canada's, almost 15,000 more babies would survive in the United States every year.

If we consider the statistics for the poor, which in the United States have been classified by race, we find that in 2001, infants born of black mothers were dying at a rate of 14.2 per thousand. That's a Third World figure, comparable to Russia's.

But now that the United States has begun to do studies based on income levels instead of race, these "cultural" and genetic explanations are turning out to be baseless. Infant mortality is highest among the poor, regardless of race.

Vive la Différence!

Genetically, Canadians and Americans are quite similar. Our health habits, too, are very much alike—people in both countries eat too much and exercise too little. And, like the United States, there is plenty of inequality in Canada, too. In terms of health care, that inequality falls primarily on Canadians in isolated communities, particularly Native groups, who have poorer access to medical care and are exposed to greater environmental contamination. The only major difference between the two countries that could account for the remarkable disparity in their infant and adult mortality rates, as well as the amount they spend on health care, is how they manage their health care systems.

The facts are clear: Before 1971, when both countries had similar, largely privately funded health care systems overall survival and mortality rates were almost identical. The divergence appeared with the introduction of the single-payer health systems in Canada.

The solid statistics amassed since the 1970s point to only one conclusion: like it or not, believe it makes sense or not, publicly funded, universally available health care is simply the most powerful contributing factor to the overall health of the people who live in any country. And in the United States, we have got the bodies to prove it.

| *"The verdict: Canadians pay more for their health care and get less."*

Canada's Health Care Is Not a Good System

Doug Wilson

Doug Wilson is an author and a commentator. In the following viewpoint, he argues that the US health care system is superior to the Canadian system. Wilson concludes that Canadians pay more and get less when it comes to health care: Canada has reduced the number of various types of health professionals, limited the availability of advanced equipment, and restricted prescription drug choices.

As you read, consider the following questions:

1. How many registered US voters stated that health care was important to their vote?

2. How do Canadians pay more for their health care?

3. According to the author, how do Canadian doctors feel about the amount of time Canadian patients are forced to wait for many treatments and procedures?

Doug Wilson, "What Canada Can Tell Us About Government Health Care," Townhall.com, February 25, 2008. Reprinted with permission.

Americans may not agree on much between now and November [2008], but we have reached a consensus about
the importance of at least one issue: health care.

In a recent study by the Pew Research Center, 76 percent
of registered voters said that health care was very important to
their vote. Democrats ranked health care their most important
issue; Independents slotted it as their second most important
issue. Republicans, meanwhile, positioned health care as more
important than social issues such as abortion, gay marriage
and stem cell research.

This public concern has prompted political action—or at
least political posturing. It seems every politician has a plan to
solve our health care woes. For Democrats, the silver bullet remains universal, government-funded coverage. Both Senators
[Barack] Obama and [Hillary] Clinton have proposed regula-
tion and tax-heavy programs to offer cradle-to-grave health
care for Americans.

Ironically, these proposals come at a time when some of
our other entitlements—Social Security and Medicare—stand
on the brink of collapse. For example, most experts agree that
Social Security will be entirely bankrupt by 2041, and that the
system will show serious financial strain as early as 2017. If a
business faced such dire financial straits it would cut costs,
but the government continues its perpetual spending spree.

Is Another Entitlement Program Desirable?

Before we allow the government to burden us with another
mammoth entitlement program, however, we might well consider the plight of countries currently employing socialized
medicine. And we need not look very far for an example.
Since the 1960s, Canada has operated a system of socialized
medicine, while also forbidding the private sector from insur-
ing medically necessary care.

The verdict: Canadians pay more for their health care and
get less. That's according to the Fraser Institute, an indepen-

Canadian Health Care System

Maybe it was just the experiences I had, seeing a patient who had the classic symptoms of sleep apnea and needed to go to a sleep disorders clinic for a test: three-year wait list. My father, who could barely walk—classic symptoms of spinal stenosis—was told he needed an MRI and told he should wait eight or nine months.

What I discovered was how many Canadians were realizing that there was a problem in the system. Today, things are very different than they were even a short time ego. A private clinic opens up at a rate of about one a week in Canada. One of the foremost critics of Canadian health care is a doctor who was just elected president of the Canadian Medical Association. Even the Supreme Court of Canada recognizes something is desperately amiss; in 2005 they ruled that access to waiting lists is not access to health care.

David Gratzer,
"Can Capitalism Save American Health Care?"
Manhattan Institute for Policy Research, June 1, 2008.
www.manhattan-institute.org.

dent research and educational organization based in Canada. Fraser's recently released study, "Paying More, Getting Less: Measuring the Sustainability of Government Health Spending in Canada" calls our attention to the painful realities of government-funded health care.

How, exactly, do Canadians pay more for their health care? Taxes, naturally—and higher and higher ones at that, for there is no other way to maintain such an enormous entitlement. Consider that by 2035, six of 10 Canadian provinces will spend half of their taxpayer-generated revenue on health-related expenses.

In slow economic times, health spending tends to exceed revenue. The government responds by raising existing taxes or creating new ones; to do otherwise would lead to the neglect of other government programs like schools and roads.

Canadian Health Care

By restricting the market, public health care programs create long waits for specialists and often prevent patients from pursuing new treatments. Indeed, the median wait times between a referral from a family or general doctor to a specialist for further treatment increased significantly in every Canadian province between 1997 and 2006. For many treatments and procedures, Canadians are forced to wait twice as long as doctors believe is medically advisable.

Canada's restrictive policies have also reduced the number of various types of health professionals, limited the availability of advanced equipment and severely restricted the prescription drug choices. Consider that even after Health Canada certifies a new drug, it takes over a year for that drug to actually reach the patients who need it. Between 2004 and 2005, it took an average of 439 days for provinces to receive reimbursement for drugs, forcing patients to wait months for necessary medications.

The list could go on, but it need not. We get the picture. The question is: What are we going to do about it?

"*Quebec should recognize that its history of cultural survival is a subject of pride, and that its self-emancipation in the Quiet Revolution has largely failed.*"

Quebec Separatism Is a Dead Issue

Conrad Black

Conrad Black is a historian, writer, and publisher. In the following viewpoint, he states that "the Quebec nationalists have had a long run, but the audience has gone from the theatre, the music has stopped, and the lights are out." Black also contends that the rest of Canada has tired of Quebec's constant calls of victimization and independence.

As you read, consider the following questions:

1. According to Black, how would the American Revolution have ended without French intervention?

2. What is the achievement of the Roman Catholic Church in Quebec, according to Black?

3. What has Quebec's political acuity accomplished, according to Black?

Conrad Black, "Quebec Is a Bore," *National Post*, December 19, 2009. Reprinted with permission.

In perhaps the greatest moment of his meteoric career, Claude Wagner—Quebec's justice minister, twice a judge, federal MP [member of Parliament], runner-up to Robert Bourassa as Quebec Liberal leader in 1970 and to Joe Clark as federal Progressive Conservative leader in 1976—electrified the Quebec Liberal convention that was choosing a successor to Jean Lesage four decades ago: "We must look ourselves in the eye and say what must be said." He did so, but the fix was in from Ottawa, and the Lesage liberals and Wagner came second, ahead of Pierre Laporte, who was murdered nine months later in the FLQ crisis [the Front de Libération du Québec, an organization promoting an independent and socialist Quebec, kidnapped and killed Quebec Minister of Labour Pierre Laporte in October 1970].

The Truth About Quebec Separatism

It is surely time, 40 years on, that Quebec followed Wagner's advice. The Quebec nationalists have had a long run, but the audience has gone from the theatre, the music has stopped, and the lights are out. Maurice Duplessis and his most assiduous disciple, Daniel Johnson Sr., were the only Quebec leaders who managed to get the province's conservatives and nationalists to vote together, an artistic political achievement. Duplessis said the Quebec nationalists are a "10-pound fish on a five-pound line; you have to reel them in slowly and let them out slowly." Johnson said: "We must give Ottawa every kick except the last one."

Duplessis told his cabinet in 1958: "I shut the nationalists up for 10 years by giving Quebec a flag. I can shut them up for another 10 years by opening a Quebec office in Paris," (which he was prepared to do when [Charles] de Gaulle returned to power and dispensed with the Fourth Republic, which Duplessis, who served continuously as premier of Quebec from before that Republic was founded to after it collapsed some twenty governments later, regarded as a farce).

"And I will shut them down for 10 years after that by giving them a world's fair. Then you will be on your own. Someone will take my place but you will not replace me."

This was pretty much what happened, except that Duplessis died a decade early, and his chosen successors, Paul Sauvé and Daniel Johnson, who had most of Duplessis's strengths and few of his shortcomings, but lacked his stamina, died in their early 50s, in office, Johnson in 1968, less than a year after the close of the Montreal World's Fair.

The nationalist torch in Quebec passed to René Lévesque and the left. But it was still a confidence trick. The 1980 and 1995 referendum questions were bogus requests for a mandate to negotiate "sovereignty" while maintaining "association"; eat the cake but still have it before you to contemplate in salivary self-irrigation.

And it was a farce. The great architect of the new nation, Claude Morin, proved to be a federal government double agent; the parliamentary leader was caught trying to flee on foot after shoplifting at Eaton's. Lévesque himself ran down and killed a derelict in the middle of the night while apparently coming off a boozy evening, and the police conveniently took five hours or more before the thought of a breathalyzer popped into mind.

The Revolution Has Failed

Now the pitiful detritus of the independentists are advocating revocation of the right of Quebec parents to chose the language of their children's daycare centres, as if the English language were a primitive dialect of no legal standing and not the language of the great majority of Canadians and Americans and a billion other people, and as if the rights of English-speaking Quebecers, exercised for centuries, could be repealed in a trice by low, delusional, separatist demagogues.

Quebec should recognize that its history of cultural survival is a subject of pride, and that its self-emancipation in the

69

Quiet Revolution has largely failed. Alone, abandoned by the French, it made its deal with the British in the Quebec Act of 1774, kept the French language, and sent Benjamin Franklin packing when he came to rally the French-Canadians against the British in the Revolutionary War.

These events were fraught with ironies, as the Americans, despite all the claptrap about "no taxation without representation" improvised by the Boston merchants and Virginia slaveholders, were really trying to leave Britain with the entire cost of removing the French as a threat to them in the Seven Years' War. When Franklin failed to induce the former American bête noire of French Canada to throw in with the Americans, (who would have assimilated them in 10 years, no matter what guaranties they had given), he removed to Paris and, in the greatest diplomatic triumph of American history, persuaded France to go to war against Britain in favour of American democracy and anti-colonialism.

Without French intervention, the Americans could not have won, and France would probably not have had their own revolution. The Americans ditched the French as soon as Britain offered acceptable terms. In the whole swirling drama, the French Canadians were the only player that acted with wisdom (unlike the British and French), and integrity (unlike the Americans). These facts should be celebrated in Quebec.

The achievement of the Roman Catholic Church in building and retaining a high literacy rate, a competitive health care system, the French culture (albeit a rustic version of it), and a birth rate that ensured French Quebec's demographic survival for 200 years, was an astounding feat. That too should be celebrated.

Assessing the Duplessis Legacy

On the 50th anniversary of his death, in September [2009], Maurice Duplessis was largely remembered as a tenebrous and primitive retardant to Quebec's progress. In fact, he was the

Poll Finds Sovereignty to Be a Dead Issue

Thirty years after the 1980 referendum and fifteen years after 1995 [the second referendum on Quebec separating from Canada], a 58% majority of Quebecers feels that the Quebec sovereignty debate is settled, while a 26% minority believes it is more relevant than ever.

Federal Idea,
"Survey: 30 Years After the 1980 Referendum,
Quebecers Believe the Issue Is Outmoded," May 18, 2010.
http://ideefederale.ca.

saviour of Quebec's jurisdiction and the physical modernizer of the province. He recouped Quebec's forfeited right to collect income taxes, and reasserted the provinces' constitutionally guaranteed concurrent right to direct taxation. His government built 3,000 schools, all the universities except McGill; the autoroutes; extended electricity to 97% of rural Quebec; made Quebec Canada's leader in disability pensions and daycare access; attracted huge investments in the mining, manufacturing, and forest products industries, while reducing taxes and eliminating debt. Quebec's per capita income gained on English Canada's for the only time in the country's history.

Duplessis did this by retaining clerical personnel in the schools and hospitals at a fraction of what secular personnel would have had to be paid, and without the disruptions of unionization and endless strikes in the public services, or the bane of schoolteachers' unions insisting on a complete separation of scholastic performance from teachers' pay scales.

Duplessis's Quebec was priest-ridden and his government was heavy-handed and cynical, though unsanctimonious, and enlivened by its leader's lively sense of humour. He had the genius of maximizing the interests of French Quebec without oppressing its minorities or threatening the integrity of Canada. This too, should be celebrated.

The Quiet Revolution which followed has been the greatest orgy of self-serving myth-making in Canadian history. The teachers and nurses left their religious orders and performed the same tasks as before, less assiduously and at 10 times the cost to Quebec's taxpayers. Almost all manufacturing and almost a million Quebecers have fled, and unknowable billions of investment dollars have avoided the province. The birth rate has collapsed. This should not be celebrated, but in the perversity of Quebec's disorientation, it is.

It all went horribly wrong when English Canada responded to the sentiment expressed by Quebec's nationalist leader in the thirties, Dr. Philippe Hamel, (before Duplessis evicted him from public life and sent him back to the practice of dentistry): "Conquer us with goodwill, my English-Canadian friends. You will be astonished at the easy victory which awaits you." The Laurendeau-Dunton commission was established and its recommendations were followed. French and English were established on an equal footing throughout the country, at considerable inconvenience and expense to the majority.

Quebec Is a Spoiled Bore

The federal government poured money raised in the wealthy English provinces into Quebec, and the response of the heirs of Hamel and Duplessis and of the Quebec cultural and political elite generally, was to accuse Canada of attempting to assimilate French Quebec. All English-Canadian political leaders since [Lester] Pearson and [Robert] Stanfield have had nothing but goodwill for Quebec. But, as one of Canada's greatest and most generous-minded modern political leaders, John P. Robarts, told me in 1977 about the then current Quebec leaders, "What spoiled child when offered chocolate ice cream, won't ask for vanilla; and how do you reach agreement with people who don't want to reach an agreement?" You don't and we didn't.

Haitians and North Africans, who haven't the remotest interest in Quebec nationalism, are being imported to replace the unborn, in an effort to maintain francophone numbers. But Quebec is superannuated, both as bully and as cry baby. No one wants to hear it anymore. There is no significant ill will to Quebec in English-Canada, but the province's ability to frighten or perplex the country, or even arouse its curiosity, is past. Quebec is a bore.

The description of French Canadians in [Louis] Hémon's *Maria Chapdelaine* as 'a race that knows not how to die' was accurate in the era described, 100 years ago. Now, that is almost all Québécois do know.

Quebec's political acuity enabled it to exercise an influence in Canada beyond its numerical strength for the first 135 years of Confederation, reaping the reward of the 10 generations of survivalist forbearance of its ancestors. It should now do homage to its honourable past, stop pretending that the lights went on only in 1960, forsake infantilism (like sending 50 separatist MPs to Ottawa to mock federalism and vest their pensions) and enjoy Quebec's earned and potential status in what—despite the purblind malice of the separatists, who habitually claim English Canada to be a pathetic excrescence of the anglo-Americans—has become one of the most successful countries in the world.

"*If Quebec sovereignty is the ultimate goal and that is the will of Quebecers, it's a good idea to start talking about it now.*"

Quebec Separatism Is Still a Viable Issue

CK

CK is a bureaucrat, blogger, and political commentator. In the following viewpoint, CK discerns a renewal of interest behind the Quebec sovereignty movement, or separatist movement. CK examines the politics behind the movement, assesses its chances of success, and delineates the major obstacles to progress.

As you read, consider the following questions:

1. According to CK, who should Quebecers look to if they want to talk about reviving Quebec sovereignty?

2. How does Pauline Marois employ the environment to inspire support for Quebec sovereignty?

3. What does CK see as the biggest obstacle to achieving Quebec separatism peacefully?

CK, "Quebec Sovereignty Movement Making a Comeback?" *Sister Sage's Musings* (blog), February 7, 2010. Reprinted with permission.

I first caught hint of this in, oddly enough, the *Edmonton Journal*, a paper from a highly conservative province that has not only never made any secret about wanting Quebec out of Canada, but a lot of the most conservative Albertans would love to separate from Canada themselves as they seem to think Alberta and Alberta alone supports the rest of Canada.

Quebec Sovereignty coming back: wishful thinking on their (*Edmonton Journal*) part? Or is it being revived slowly for real?

The Separatist Movement Is Alive

Up until now [February 2010], the movement had been all but dead for the last few years with the exception of a few rantings from Pauline Marois [leader of Parti Québécois]. However, I never believed too many people: sovereignists (separatist) & federalists alike took her seriously nor would they consider her as premier, or worse yet, president (I'm thinking pretty good guess a sovereign Quebec would adapt a republican style of government given general Québécois disdain for the royal family). In my opinion, she only served one purpose and that was to raise the Parti Québécois [PQ, a political party that advocates Quebec sovereignty] from the dead following the disastrous performance of André Boisclair [former leader of Parti Québécois].

Oddly enough, if we want to talk about reviving Quebec sovereignty, I think more Quebecers look to Gilles Duceppe [a Quebec nationalist] than to Marois.

Gilles Duceppe's last federal election campaign had nothing to [do] with sovereignty; wasn't on his campaign platform. He basically campaigned on that he was the best choice to keep Stevie [Stephen Harper] and his neocon ways out of Quebec as much as possible. Jean Charest, our federalist premier and a former federal Tory himself campaigned for the Bloc Québécois [BQ]. A lot of my English speaking friends and co-workers even voted for the Bloc Québécois knowing full well that they were a sovereignist party but having a distaste for the Liberals' bad choices for leaders since [former Canadian prime minister] Paul Martin and for Stevie, a sovereignist party seemed more palpable.

Duceppe Talks Sovereignty

The twentieth anniversary of the fall of the Meech Lake Accord [failed amendments to the Canadian Constitution] happens this coming June [2010] and guess where Gilles Duceppe has been recently? Pitching sovereignty at University of Ottawa. Sounds like an odd place to promote sovereignty to me. Hell, even Concordia or McGill would have made more sense as venues for that. Be that as it may, Duceppe spoke of Meech and launched into a speech before the students.

> "It is clear that in Canada there is no political will to respond to Quebec's aspirations."

Of course, it didn't take all that long for Marois to jump on Duceppe's bandwagon. She says that a sovereign Quebec would be more green than if it remains with Canada.

> "Quebec is a leader (on environmental issues) . . . and Canada, for its part, is dragging us down."

I wouldn't argue that it isn't Quebec's intent to be green and to set targets. However, can this be done only in a sovereign Quebec? That is just one question.

> "Since 1990, Quebec has made considerable efforts to attack greenhouse gas emissions, and suddenly they (in Ottawa) change the reference year for calculating those reductions. Who do you think will pay for this? Quebec's citizens, companies and workers," Marois said.

> "If we were independent tomorrow, we could speak with our own voice. We would not have been feuding in Copenhagen. We could have signed the Kyoto agreement ourselves.

"This is the demonstration that federalism does not suit the Quebec reality. Whether we have governments that are in one case federalist and the other sovereignist, we always come to the same conclusion: This federalism is impossible to reform, and the real solution for Quebec is sovereignty."

She made these remarks the day after Charest accused [Minister of the Environment Jim] Prentice of spreading falsehoods about Quebec's new restrictions on vehicle emissions. Basically, Jim Prentice ridiculed Charest.

The environment is but one issue Marois is using to promote sovereignty. Quebec is still not in the Canadian Constitution to this day and not likely to become a part of it anytime soon.

A Renewed Push

The Bloc and PQ both plan to springboard activities toward the commemoration of the death anniversary of Meech Lake leading toward a renewed push for sovereignty, but not before one more set of negotiations for more powers over such things as culture, language, and environment and if those demands are not met, Alexandre Cloutier, PQ critic of intergovernmental affairs, seems to think that it will make it easier to get support for outright independence. It gives me the idea of an ultimatum to be served up to Ottawa: give us the autonomy we're asking or we're gone. I think we can all guess how that will turn out.

Right now, CROP and Léger Marketing polls indicate a tie between Charest and Marois with Charest's numbers going down, largely in part because he is refusing to hold a public inquiry into allegations of corruption and price-rigging in the rewarding of public construction contracts. His numbers can continue to go down, however, given he won a majority in the last provincial election in 2008, Charest is not expected to call an election anytime soon, might not even happen for a few years yet, unless, of course, he is forced to resign, but in absence of anyone suitable to take over the Quebec Liberal party, that is not likely to happen for the time being.

Politics Matter

However, if Quebec sovereignty is the ultimate goal and that is the will of Quebecers, it's a good idea to start talking about it now. Perhaps even answer serious questions. I have the feeling that the 'yes' side (PQ, Bloc and other sovereignists) can't even agree on how to achieve this. For starters, in spite of the fact the ADQ [Action démocratique du Québec] is all but dead, sovereignists, including those in the Parti Québécois themselves are clearly divided right/left: the left being mainly out of Montreal and the right being pretty much everywhere else, including Quebec City. How else did Harpercons win as many seats as they did in the province of Quebec? I would hazard a guess that those voters are not necessarily federalist but they do support that right-wing agenda. These folks are socially conservative for the most part.

Michel Bolduc, the blogger of *Chronicles of a Pure Laine* seems to believe that sovereignty can be achieved peacefully. As someone who has travelled extensively across Quebec and having lived in both rural towns and in Montreal, I would have to disagree. But not due to English/French war or the division of east/west Montreal or anything like that. The problem would be a Montreal v. the rest of Quebec (particularly rural Quebec). I remembered living in Lac-Mégantic with my ex-husband for a few years: His family as well as a lot of the inhabitants didn't like me. Not because I was English speaking; my French was just fine for them, in fact, they never thought I was Anglophone until I told them much much later on: They thought I was either Acadian from New Brunswick or from the Gaspésie. They hated the fact that I was the big city girl from Montreal with my 'airs of superiority'. While most of the inhabitants of Mégantic and outskirts didn't have a postsecondary education, they had a basic distrust of my educational background.

I have also spent time in many other rural towns in Quebec from Gaspésie to Outaouais; from Lac-St-Jean to Abitibi. I had varying degrees of the same reaction when they found out I was from Montreal.

Please note that I am not speaking of everybody who lives in rural Quebec; I'm speaking of my observations in general after having spent time with them.

Montreal is generally more progressive. When pundits speak of Quebecers being more supportive of keeping the gun registry than the rest of Canada (for the most part), more supportive of strong social programs, more environmentally conscious; they tend to think of only Montrealers and forget about rural Quebecers.

Rural Quebecers (from my observations) tend to be more influenced by the local Catholic Church in their town; thus would [be] against things like same-sex marriage and legalized abortions. They are avid hunters, thus, unfortunately, they support scrapping the long gun registry. A lot of them are on farms or in a house on land that belonged to their families for generations. In spite of chronic unemployment issues in certain regions, most are absolutely against the welfare state. One can hear them bitching about how they're breaking their backs working so hard in the woods, farms or factories only to pay taxes to support lazy welfare recipients. While Montreal mayor, Gérald Tremblay wanted to put a ban on fireplaces and woodstoves given the air generated into the atmosphere is considered pollution, many rural Quebecers use their fireplaces and wood stoves and I would dare anyone to try to take them away.

They also tend to be a lot less tolerant of immigrants than in Montreal. Remember Hérouxville? That small town which began that whole inquiry into reasonable accommodations by making rules about not stoning women and such [the rules were posted on the town's website in January 2007]. I always thought that was funny given that I don't think there are too many immigrants and certainly no Muslims in Hérouxville and surrounding areas, but, I digress.

Who Would Lead Quebec?

Furthermore, who would be suitable to not only lead the PQ in the next election but essentially, be president of a newly sovereign Quebec? I certainly wouldn't trust Marois. Let's remember that she wasn't a great finance minister and that she did buy off doctors' contracts for them to retire and she closed down quite a few hospitals. I know, right-leaning Federal Liberals cut transfer payments to the provinces leading to cuts in services, including health care in all of Canada, but Marois could have cut other things elsewhere. It only proved her shortsightedness. Recently, she made a blunder for which she had to correct shortly after. She had said that she would have made those same cuts again today. If she were leading a sovereign Quebec, I have my doubts about it remaining as progressive as many would like to think.

Economically, Quebec is a have-not province and has been for a long time. It has a steep deficit like that of the other provinces. I wonder how that would be financed? How would they (gov't of a sovereign Quebec) correct a chronic unemployment problem in some of the regions like Gaspésie or Lac-St-Jean? Granted, I believe they would start by collecting the taxes we would always pay to the federal government, but is that enough?

Imagining a Sovereign Quebec

Then what would a sovereign Quebec mean? A partnership with Canada of some kind, say like what Puerto Rico is the U.S.? Or the outright country of Quebec? Would they sign on to NAFTA [North American Free Trade Agreement] (I would hope not; a sure way of a sovereign Quebec not escaping from having an American health care system or more of the same issues as with softwood lumber among other issues)?

So many questions. [In his October 25, 2009, blog post,] Michel Bolduc attempts to explain Quebec separation, answering some common questions. Some of his answers to some questions make sense, but there are others that concern me such as health care, NAFTA, employment opportunities and economy. However, I would venture a guess that a sovereign Quebec would be more palpable than a Harpercon majority, but not by much.

For me, the priority is to make sure Stevie never ever gets his precious majority and hopefully, he and his nasty little evengelical Harpercon flunkies also go away; after all, another federal election is going to happen long before a provincial election in Quebec and for right now, we have a federalist premier leading a federalist party for better or for worse and thus, a joint PQ and BQ effort at playing constitutional hardball with Ottawa, thus leading to yet another referendum on sovereignty is a long way off. After Stevie and his nasty friends are gone (a girl can hope), I would like to see some of these questions about what a sovereign Quebec would be like answered and what kind of compromises can be made between Montreal and the rest of Quebec.

Periodical and Internet Sources Bibliography

The following articles have been selected to supplement the diverse views presented in this chapter.

Kalli Anderson	"Meech Lake Is Dead. Long Live Meech Lake," *Globe and Mail*, June 22, 2010.
Mona Charen	"About Canada—Health Care and More," Townhall.com, August 18, 2009. http://townhall.com.
Kevin Dougherty	"PQ Setting Stage for Another Run at Sovereignty," *Gazette* (Montreal), June 19, 2010.
Meagan Fitzpatrick	"Keep Canadians in Loop on Health-Care Spending," *National Post*, August 24, 2010.
Gazette (Montreal)	"Hacking Away at Freedom—PQ Style," June 25, 2010.
David Gratzer	"Canada's ObamaCare Precedent," *Wall Street Journal*, June 9, 2009.
Sarah Hampson	"Pauline Marois: The Softer, Gentler Face of Quebec Sovereignty," *Globe and Mail*, October 27, 2008.
David Johnston	"Kosovo Isn't a Precedent for Separation: Rae," *Gazette* (Montreal), August 21, 2010.
Naomi Lakritz	"Some Good and Bad News Out of Quebec," *Calgary Herald*, June 23, 2010.
Shaun Polczer	"Alberta Looks to Balance Oilsands, Environment," *Calgary Herald*, August 27, 2010.
Colin Robertson	"Let's Act Like an Energy Superpower," *Globe and Mail*, July 27, 2010.
David Ker Thomson	"Against Canada," *CounterPunch*, February 12–14, 2010.

OPPOSING
VIEWPOINTS®
SERIES

CHAPTER 2

What Are the Major Foreign Policy Issues in Canada?

Chapter Preface

In 1969 the US supertanker SS *Manhattan* traveled through the Northwest Passage, a sea route through the Arctic Ocean connecting the Atlantic and Pacific oceans. The huge ship was testing a route for the shipment of Alaskan crude oil and was fitted with special equipment to break the thick ice. The supertanker made it through, but it took months to repair the damage done to the ship.

Environmentalists were outraged at the potential damage an oil spill could do in the pristine Arctic waters. Canadian politicians were also alarmed at the implications. They passed the Arctic Waters Pollution Prevention Act, which allowed Canada to control navigation in waters extending 161 kilometers offshore. Canada was decisively asserting its sovereignty over the Northwest Passage.

In 1985 the United States challenged Canadian sovereignty over the Northwest Passage again. An American ship called the USCGC *Polar Sea* embarked on a trip through the Northwest Passage without asking permission, ignoring Canadian sovereignty claims. The United States argued that it didn't need permission because it was an international waterway. The incident led to an Arctic cooperation agreement, which required the United States to seek consent from Canada to send any more icebreakers through the passage.

In recent years, a contentious debate over control of the major Arctic waterways has been thrust once again to the forefront of international politics. Now that it is clear that the Arctic has valuable mineral and energy resources yet to be mined, both Russia and the United States are suddenly eager to stake their claim in the region. In addition, they argue that the Northwest Passage is an international strait that should be open to all international travel. With the effects of global warming, experts predict that the Northwest Passage could be free of ice for large parts of the summer in fifteen years, allowing regular travel in the waterway. The Northwest Passage will suddenly become a hot destination for international shipping: It would knock 3,100 miles off the current shipping route through the Panama Canal.

To make an airtight legal case of Canadian sovereignty of Arctic waters, Canada must prove two things: The waters must be shown to be the internal waters of Canada and that the Northwest Passage is not an international passage. Canada argues that it can meet both of these requirements. Canada also asserts that many of the Arctic waterways, including the Northwest Passage, are frozen over most of the year and can be considered an extension of the land, thereby establishing its sovereignty over the entire area. In recent years, the Canadian government has turned its attention to its northern territories, pledging to build a deep-water port and establish an Arctic warfare training center. The government has also bought several patrol ships for enforcing Canadian control over the waterways.

With the melting of the ice caused by climate change, however, Canadian jurisdiction over the region is bound to be challenged again. Shipping routes will be open longer, allowing more large tankers and military ships to travel through a very important waterway. With Russia, the United States, and other northern countries making claims on Arctic resources such as oil, natural gas, and minerals, and in need of a cost-efficient shipping route, the debate over Canadian sovereignty over Arctic waterways will stay a relevant and contentious issue for the years to come.

The topic of Canadian sovereignty over the Arctic straits is examined in the following chapter, which explores some of the key foreign policy issues in Canada in recent years. Viewpoints included in this chapter also debate the Canadian military effort in Afghanistan and the nation's foreign aid budget and allocation.

> "With Americans leery of the troop in-
> creases that go along with counterin-
> surgency, many, including some influ-
> ential senators like Carl Levin, are
> considering a more Canadian approach
> focused on quickly scaling up the Af-
> ghan army and police force."

Canadian Military Efforts in Afghanistan Are Laudable

Tim Fernholz

Tim Fernholz is a research fellow at the New America Founda-
tion and a writer for the American Prospect. *In the following*
viewpoint, he describes the different approaches of the American
and Canadian military forces in fighting the war in Afghanistan.
Fernholz argues that many in the American government are
coming around to the Canadian way of thinking and admire the
Canadian way of doing things.

As you read, consider the following questions:

1. How many troops has Canada committed to the Afghanistan war through 2011?

Tim Fernholz, "The Canadian Way of War," *The American Prospect*, November 13, 2009.
Reprinted with permission.

2. In what Afghanistan city were the Canadian forces essentially on their own until 2008?

3. How does Fernholz characterize the Canadian approach to fighting the war in Afghanistan?

It was a public relations stunt worthy of P.T. Barnum [19th-century showman and promoter] perfect for getting the attention of an uninterested American audience: Tuck an Afghan village, complete with authentic Afghans, into the heart of Washington, D.C., right between the White House and Capitol Hill. Then, blow it the hell up.

The most surprising part of the whole idea was who came up with it: the Canadian government.

Boom!

Alas, sober-minded authorities managed to shut down this worthwhile Canadian initiative a few days before it occurred, thinking the melodramatics might frighten citizens still trained by the [George W.] Bush administration to panic at the slightest whiff of terrorism. The staff of the Canadian embassy, where the staged attack was set to take place, elected to soldier on with a decidedly less flashy forum designed to remind Americans that Canadians are still fighting alongside—and, for a time, were fighting without—U.S. troops in Afghanistan.

An Interesting Gathering

The Canadian embassy is an expansive limestone structure, modernist in style, beautiful to approach, and apparently an architectural joke on us—an anecdote from the biography of the designer, Arthur Erickson, reports that the zoning-mandated columns in the facade are hollow, "mocking the U.S. and all of its imperial pretensions." Maybe so, but it's the little touches—like the sign by the fountain informing passersby of "eau non potable"—that retain an air of Canadian punctiliousness.

Inside, instead of Afghans and pyrotechnics, I found an assemblage of Canadian officials, an assortment of representatives from other NATO [North Atlantic Treaty Organization] allies, and even a bagpipe player flown in from Montreal specifically for the event. But scant few Americans were in attendance. Following a couple of Canadian military officers who joked about their need for a drink—"It's the Afghanistan effect!"—I ran into Jennie Chen, an embassy counselor who had just returned from a year-long diplomatic stint in Afghanistan. The conflict, she said, is a big issue in Canada, which has committed some 2,700 troops through 2011. Canadians, she explained, emphasize a whole-of-government approach, primarily focused on developing the Afghan army rather than engaging in the kind of counterinsurgency operations now popular in the U.S. military.

"We welcome the U.S.," Chen said of the recent American troop deployments to Afghanistan, "particularly in the south— we've been holding it on our own."

Indeed, around Kandahar, in southern Afghanistan, the Canadians were essentially on their own until last year [2008] as they attempted to train new Afghan forces and conduct security patrols of the surrounding area but lacked the troops and direction to pursue a counterinsurgency strategy of fighting to protect civilians. The Taliban [a militant Islamic fundamentalist movement] gained ground in the south—its traditional ethnic home—against frustrated Canadian forces.

"[Americans] need to understand this is the toughest environment," Canadian Capt. Chris Blouin told a McClatchy reporter over the summer. "Expect everything."

A Canadian Approach

American military observers have looked down upon the work of our NATO allies in Afghanistan, deriding them for failing to leave their bases and engage the enemy "outside the wire." (Indeed, a decision by German military officers to attack suspected Taliban with missiles instead of troops led to over a hundred civilian casualties and a major public relations debacle.) They say the Canadians are better than most but still fault their ability to go after insurgents.

Now, though, with Americans leery of the troop increases that go along with counterinsurgency, many, including some influential senators like Carl Levin, are considering a more Canadian approach focused on quickly scaling up the Afghan army and police force. With public support for the war falling, policy makers in Washington are rethinking the fundamental logic of our efforts in Afghanistan and asking whether we need a counterinsurgency mission to fulfill a counterterrorism objective. It's a shame none of them made it to the forum.

One person who isn't reconsidering the American deployment is Said T. Jawad, the Afghan ambassador to the U.S. who spoke at the luncheon, glossing over recent problems with electoral fraud that put his job in jeopardy and thanking the Canadians and Americans for their sacrifices. Unless they continued, he said, terrorism would land at their doors. "I disagree with those who argue that it is dangerous to be in Afghanistan," he said. "It's a lot more dangerous not being there."

A Fundamental Difference in Approaches

The difference between the U.S. and Canadian approaches became clearer in an afternoon panel on policing, when Tom Schrettner, a Drug Enforcement Administration [DEA] agent, gave a presentation on his agency's efforts to fight drug trafficking in Afghanistan. It began a little above my head—"as you know, the major compound you need to make heroin is acetic anhydride"—but quickly came down to earth as Agent Schrettner discussed how the DEA has trained Afghans to assault suspected drug havens.

"Those sites are actioned through a military means to deprive the enemy of that resource," he explained with bureaucratic clarity. Later, he was even blunter. "There will invariably be huge gunfights."

Rebuilding Afghanistan

Canada's efforts in Afghanistan are guided by the Afghanistan Compact, a five-year blueprint for coordinating the work of the Afghan government and 60 United Nations and international partners in the areas of development, governance, and security. . . .

Canada is supporting projects that will strengthen democratic development and build public institutions in Afghanistan. Reliable community-based policing systems, building the capacity of judges and lawyers and a corrections system that meets international standards are also key components of building the legitimacy of the Afghan government.

> *Government of Canada,*
> *"Rebuilding Afghanistan," 2010.*
> *www.afghanistan.gc.ca.*

Agent Schrettner was excited to play a clip from ABC News showing a DEA team leading the Afghan police on a raid of suspected drug producers. "This will wake you up," he promised. On-screen, as police arrest a suspect, the narrator observes that though the man tells his wife and children he is only being taken for questioning, Afghanistan's harsh drug laws will put him in jail for 15 years.

It didn't seem like anyone was winning hearts and minds.

Agent Schrettner's counterpart, Paul Young of the Royal Canadian Mounted Police—sporting a standard police uniform rather than a red Dudley Do-Right getup—made a much less sexy presentation focused on training Afghanistan's regular police force. "My heart is in Afghanistan," he explained. "Parts of it have never returned." Then, with a note of reproach in his voice, he commented on the DEA presentation:

"I often wonder if we're creating a civilian police force or a paramilitary police force." There was no doubt which he preferred.

The two men then joined an Afghan general and his interpreter for a panel discussion, which offered a taste of what both nations must be going through in Afghanistan every day—even without the benefit of a fake Afghan village and a staged explosion. Doctrinal differences in the two police approaches faded to the background as both men struggled to communicate with the irascible general, who seemed to be asking if they visited Kabul's red-light district. The interpreter intervened, explaining that "he is a policeman; he doesn't go there."

The general gestured broadly—*of course* they don't get it, then.

> "Military assaults against the poverty-stricken farmers of Afghanistan and Haiti, and an Iraqi population struggling for its very survival, are part of a long, barbarous tradition going back to slave ships and colonial resource wars."

Canada Should Pull Its Troops Out of Afghanistan

David Orchard

David Orchard is the author of The Fight for Canada: Four Centuries of Resistance to American Expansionism. *In the following viewpoint, he questions Canada's involvement in the Afghanistan war, viewing it as a form of colonialism. Orchard maintains that Canadians must demand that Canada's government pull its troops from the conflict.*

As you read, consider the following questions:

1. What does the author think "waging war with bombs and guns" is accomplishing in Afghanistan?

2. How has the war affected Afghanistan's opium trade?

3. What province led the opposition to Canadian participation in the Boer War?

David Orchard, "Canada in Afghanistan," *CounterPunch*, February 26, 2008. Reprinted with permission.

The [Stephen] Harper government is seeking to prolong Canada's military involvement in Afghanistan. So far, Canada has spent six years, billions of dollars, 78 young lives (many more wounded) and inflicted unknown casualties on that country.

The terms used to describe our occupation and ongoing war are remarkably similar to those used over a century ago by colonial powers to justify their ruthless wars of colonization. Then, it was the white man's burden to "civilize" the non-whites of the Americas, Africa and Asia. As cub scouts we were taught [British writer Rudyard] Kipling's unforgettable prose about the "lesser breeds," but nothing about the real people who paid horrendous costs in death, suffering, destruction and theft of their land and resources.

War Has Consequences

Today, we are involved in a "mission" in Afghanistan to "improve" the lives of women and children, to instill "democracy," to root out corruption and the drug trade.

Waging war with bombs and guns is not helping women or instilling democracy. It is, however, strengthening the Afghan resistance—hence our increasingly shrill cries for more help from NATO [North Atlantic Treaty Organization].

The U.S. is involved in a similar "mission" in Iraq. So far, over a million Iraqis—many of them children—have died, some two million have fled the country, another two million are "internally displaced," untold hundreds of thousands wounded in an endless war waged by the world's most advanced military almost entirely against civilians.

The toll of dead, wounded and displaced for Afghanistan is not being published.

The deadly effects of radioactive, depleted uranium (DU) ammunition being inflicted on both countries (some originally from Saskatchewan) haven't begun to be tabulated or

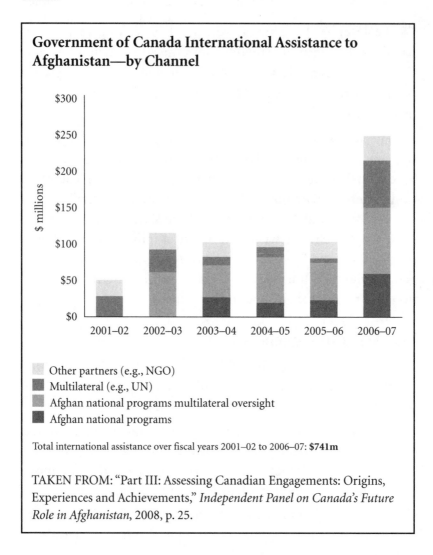

Government of Canada International Assistance to Afghanistan—by Channel

Other partners (e.g., NGO)
Multilateral (e.g., UN)
Afghan national programs multilateral oversight
Afghan national programs

Total international assistance over fiscal years 2001–02 to 2006–07: **$741m**

TAKEN FROM: "Part III: Assessing Canadian Engagements: Origins, Experiences and Achievements," *Independent Panel on Canada's Future Role in Afghanistan*, 2008, p. 25.

understood, let alone reported back to us. The idea that bombing the population will improve the lives of women and children could only come from those who have never experienced war.

As for narcotics, in 2001, when the West's attack on Afghanistan began, its opium trade was approaching eradication. Today, Afghanistan produces over 90% of the world's heroin and the U.S. is proposing mass aerial spraying of pesticides.

Remembering Vietnam

Those of the writer's generation and older will remember the U.S. onslaught against little Vietnam—the long unspeakable war—which left six million Vietnamese, Laotians and Cambodians dead, wounded or deformed.

In that extraordinary country one sees miles upon miles of neat graves in the cemeteries, thousands of acres—aerial sprayed with horrific chemicals—still lying waste, craters left from ten million tons of bombs dropped, hand excavated underground tunnels in which the people were forced to live for years on end. An ancient African saying goes, "the axe forgets, but not the tree." Today, over four million Vietnamese still suffer, many indescribably so, the effects of Agent Orange [a chemical used in herbicidal warfare in Vietnam] and other chemicals, and genetic damage is continuing from generation to generation.

In the case of Vietnam, Canada kept its troops out. Over the past decade, however, Canada has bombed Yugoslavia, helped overthrow Jean-Bertrand Aristide's democratically elected government in Haiti, is occupying Afghanistan and now, we learn, is getting involved more deeply in the U.S. devastation of Iraq. (Something Stephen Harper [prime minister of Canada] and Stockwell Day [a member of Parliament] openly advocated from the beginning of the U.S. "Shock and Awe" assault on that defenceless nation.)

Humanitarian Intervention Is Colonialism

What gives the rich, powerful, white West the right to wage unending, merciless wars against small, largely non-white, Third World countries? (Yugoslavia, where the West invented "humanitarian" bombing was not a Third World country, but according to President Bill Clinton, it needed to accept the benefits of "globalism.") The torment of civilians being subjected to the impact of modern weaponry is rarely reported in the West. Canadians, as a matter of policy, are not informed of the number or types of casualties we have inflicted.

The modern concepts of "humanitarian intervention" and the "duty to protect" which seek to override international law and national sovereignty are, in this writer's view, simply 21st century terminology for colonization.

Military assaults against the poverty-stricken farmers of Afghanistan and Haiti, and an Iraqi population struggling for its very survival, are part of a long, barbarous tradition going back to slave ships and colonial resource wars and will some day, I believe, be seen in that context. In the meantime, the agony of millions does not reach our ears or eyes, and Prime Minister Harper is busy working the phones to shore up the U.S.-led war, seeking more troops and helicopters to "finish the job."

When Canada assisted the British Empire in the Boer War over a century ago, it was Québec that led the opposition. It was again Québec's vocal resistance—and former Prime Minister [Jean] Chrétien's attention to it—that helped keep Canada's troops out of Iraq. Today, it is up to Canadians who can feel the anguish of the Third World to speak for the voiceless against Canada's new government of would-be conquistadores.

> "We must be certain that everyone who enters our waters respects our laws and regulations, particularly those that protect the fragile Arctic environment."

Canada Has Sovereignty over the Arctic Straits

Stephen Harper

Stephen Harper is the prime minister of Canada. In the following viewpoint excerpted from a speech, he asserts Canadian sovereignty over the Arctic straits, stating that Canadian claims are rooted in history. Harper makes it very clear that his government will defend this commitment with a strong Canadian military presence.

As you read, consider the following questions:

1. How does Prime Minister Harper intend to defend Arctic sovereignty?

2. According to Harper, how far does Canadian jurisdiction extend outward into the surrounding sea?

3. Name one of the measures the Harper government is taking to assert Canadian sovereignty.

Stephen Harper, "Securing Canadian Sovereignty in the Arctic," Speech transcript, Office for the Prime Minister, August 12, 2006. Reprinted with permission.

I am very pleased to be in Iqaluit, Canada's newest capital. Your city is my first stop on my first tour of the North since becoming Prime Minister.

Over the next several days I'll be making two more stops in Nunavut: the Alert military base at the very northern tip of Canada and the new Jericho diamond mine in western Nunavut.

In addition, I'll be visiting the capitals of Yukon and the Northwest Territories, Whitehorse and Yellowknife.

I'm especially pleased to be here on Canadian Forces Day so I can observe firsthand the army, navy and air force in action at the launch of Operation Lancaster.

It is always an honour to be among the men and women of our Armed Forces again.

The Work of the Canadian Military Forces

Across the country and around the world, Canadian troops are doing vitally important work for our country.

Defending our sovereignty, protecting our national interests, helping people in dire straits and fighting for democracy, freedom and the rule of law.

As Prime Minister, one of my first actions was to visit our brave soldiers in Afghanistan.

As you know, they are doing an outstanding job, in extremely difficult and dangerous circumstances.

I also made it a priority to meet new recruits graduating from training at CFB [Canadian Forces Base] Wainwright and CFB Ottawa.

And during our recent trip to Europe and the G8 [Group of 8 industrialized nations] summit in Russia, Laureen [wife of Prime Minister Stephen Harper] and I stopped in France to pay our respects to the Canadians who fell at Vimy Ridge [a World War I battle in France].

At each stop, I saw—past and present—displays of hard work, courage and dedication to Canada.

I want you to know that our new national government is very proud of our military.

And you can count on our full support on this and all your future missions.

Operation Lancaster

Operation Lancaster is a very important exercise.

Because it demonstrates our new government's commitment to asserting Canada's sovereignty over our Arctic territory.

A commitment I made last December [2005] when I promised to ensure that Canada's jurisdiction over the islands, waterways and resources in the High Arctic is respected by all nations.

But you can't defend Arctic sovereignty with words alone.

It takes a Canadian presence on the ground, in the air and on the sea and a government that is internationally recognized for delivering on its commitments.

That's why exercises such as this one are so important.

Making Our Intentions Clear

And that's why we are being absolutely clear and forthright in all our foreign policy pronouncements.

If you want to be taken seriously by other countries, you have to say what you mean and mean what you say.

And I am here today to make it absolutely clear there is no question about Canada's Arctic border.

It extends from the northern tip of Labrador all the way up the east coast of Ellesmere Island to Alert.

Then it traces the western perimeter of the Queen Elizabeth Islands down to the Beaufort Sea.

From there it hugs the coasts of the Northwest Territories and Yukon to the Canada-U.S. border at Alaska.

All along the border, our jurisdiction extends outward 200 miles into the surrounding sea, just as it does along our Atlantic and Pacific coastlines.

No more. And no less.

Historical Basis for Sovereignty

Canada's Arctic sovereignty is firmly anchored in history.

Almost 100 years ago, in 1909, a plaque was installed on Melville Island by famed Québécois seaman Joseph Bernier, captain of the Canadian government ship *Arctic*.

It proclaimed, on the ground for the first time, Canada's sovereignty over the entire Arctic archipelago.

From the 1920s through the 1940s, the great Canadian navigator Henry Larsen patrolled our Arctic waters aboard the famous RCMP [Royal Canadian Mounted Police] schooner *St. Roch*.

Larsen's many voyages upheld the first principle of Arctic sovereignty: Use it or lose it.

Law of the Sea Treaty

In the 1980s, the Conservative government of Brian Mulroney won recognition of our Arctic possessions under international law.

Canada became one of 150 nations—including most European countries, Russia, India and China—to ratify the United Nations Convention on the Law of the Sea.

Only a handful of countries remain outside the treaty today.

I have been very clear in asserting that Canada intends to enforce its rights under the Law of the Sea.

And today I am calling on all countries to sign the treaty and join Canada and the rest of the world in respecting the rule of the Law of the Sea.

Honoring the Commitment to Arctic Sovereignty

Ladies and gentlemen, for far too long, Canadian governments have failed in their duty to rigorously enforce our sovereignty in the Arctic.

They have failed to provide enough resources to comprehensively monitor, patrol and protect our northern waters.

As a result, foreign ships may have routinely sailed through our territory without permission.

Any such voyage represents a potential threat to Canadians' safety and security.

We always need to know who is in our waters and why they're there.

We must be certain that everyone who enters our waters respects our laws and regulations, particularly those that protect the fragile Arctic environment.

Our new government will not settle for anything less.

And that's why we have already begun to take action.

Measures Will Be Taken

This month [August 2006], for the first time ever, our government began conducting pollution-detection surveillance flights over our Arctic waters.

The military exercise we are launching today will take the Canadian Navy farther North than it has been for many decades.

Meanwhile we are actively exploring options for the establishment of a deep-water port in the Arctic that will extend the navy's reach even further.

We are determined to expand the army's presence in the North by establishing a new Arctic training centre and revitalizing the Canadian Rangers.

New long-range unmanned aerial surveillance drones will provide continuous air patrols throughout the Arctic.

And finally we're looking at technologies to give Canada undersea surveillance capacity—acoustic or movement sensors to detect subs and ships in our Arctic waters.

Defending Canadian Sovereignty

Some in the opposition dismiss our focus on northern sovereignty as expensive and unnecessary.

Some have actually come to the North and suggested our plans here are a waste of money.

To that I say, government's first obligation is to defend the territorial integrity of its borders.

And this will become more important in the decades to come—because northern oil and gas, minerals and other resources of the northern frontier will become ever more valuable.

The technologies used in Arctic resource extraction and transport are increasingly sophisticated and affordable.

And the Northwest Passage is becoming more accessible every year: Some scientists even predict it will be open to year-round shipping within a decade.

In short, the economics and the strategic value of northern resource development are growing ever more attractive and critical to our nation.

And trust me, it is not only Canadians who are noticing.

Protecting Canadian Interests

It is no exaggeration to say that the need to assert our sovereignty and take action to protect our territorial integrity in the Arctic has never been more urgent.

The North is poised to take a much bigger role in Canada's economic and social development.

It is attracting international attention, investment capital, people, and commercial and industrial development.

Therefore the Government of Canada has an enormous responsibility to ensure that development occurs on our terms.

Honoring the North and Its People

In particular, we must ensure the unique ecosystem of the North, and the unique cultural traditions of the First People [native people of Canada] of the North, are respected and protected.

That's what we said we would do, and that's what we're going to do.

We want the world to know about the amazing opportunities that lie ahead for northern Canada; but let there be no misunderstanding:

This is Nunavut—"Our Land"—just as Yukon and the Northwest Territories and the entire Arctic Archipelago are "Our Land."

And, on this you have my word, we will back our sovereignty over "Our Land" with all the tools at our disposal, including the men and women of our Armed Forces who are launching Operation Lancaster from Iqaluit today.

Thank you, merci, ...

God Bless the True North, Strong and Free!

> "The Bush directive reiterates that the Northwest Passage is an international waterway—a rebuttal of Canada's claim of sovereignty over what is emerging as a major global shipping route because of the shrinking polar ice cap."

Canadian Sovereignty in the Arctic Straits Is Disputed

Mike Blanchfield and Randy Boswell

Mike Blanchfield and Randy Boswell are reporters for the Canwest News Service. In the following viewpoint, they discuss the release of a new directive on the Arctic from the George W. Bush administration that challenges Canadian sovereignty in the region. According to the directive, the United States considers the Northwest Passage and the Northern Sea Route international assets, and the United States intends to protect its access to them.

As you read, consider the following questions:

1. What are key elements of Bush's policy that challenge Canadian sovereignty?

2. What did a Russian submarine do to assert Russian sovereignty in the Arctic?

Mike Blanchfield and Randy Boswell, "Bush Asserts U.S. Sea Power over Arctic Straits," *Vancouver Sun*, October 19, 2009. Reprinted with permission.

3. According to the directive, the United States is prepared to cooperate in what bilateral settings?

In his final days in power, President George W. Bush asserted U.S. military "sea power" over the oil-rich Arctic on Monday, in another forceful rebuttal of Canada's claims of sovereignty over the Northwest Passage.

The White House formally released the text of a sweeping new directive on the Arctic, two years in the making, just eight days before Barack Obama is to be sworn in as the 44th U.S. president.

Challenging Canadian Sovereignty

Key elements of Bush's policy challenge the ambitious Arctic sovereignty agenda put forth by Prime Minister Stephen Harper that includes bolstering Canada's military presence and fostering economic and social development. The Bush directive reiterates that the Northwest Passage is an international waterway—a rebuttal of Canada's claim of sovereignty over what is emerging as a major global shipping route because of the shrinking polar ice cap—and it highlights the boundary dispute in the resource-rich Beaufort Sea.

"I think Canada has gotten a real wake-up call with this," said University of Calgary political scientist Rob Huebert, one [of] the country's leading experts on Arctic issues.

He said he couldn't recall the U.S. ever articulating its disagreements with Canada "in such black-and-white terms. There was no effort here to sugarcoat anything."

Huebert noted that the bold assertion of American interests in the Arctic came only weeks after a similar statement by European officials also posed challenges to Canada's polar strategy.

"Freedom of the seas is a top national priority," the White House directive states. "The Northwest Passage is a strait used for international navigation, and the Northern Sea Route includes straits used for international navigation. Preserving the rights and duties relating to navigation and overflight in the Arctic region supports our ability to exercise these rights throughout the world, including through strategic straits."

Fighting for Access to the North's Resources

The Arctic's untapped energy potential has sparked a 21st-century scramble in the Far North that has included a Russian submarine planting a flag on the North Pole seabed and Canada's expressions of its own Arctic aspirations under Harper, which include a greater military land and sea presence.

Despite noticeably warmer relations between Ottawa and Washington, the two governments have disagreed in the past on the environmental impact of new drilling for oil in the Arctic, as well as Canada's sovereignty claims over the Northwest Passage.

Harper's office had no immediate comment.

Bush's memorandum directs several key agencies to define the full extent of U.S. Arctic boundaries because of its "compelling interest" in the region. The policy cites climate change, defence against possible terrorist threats and "a growing awareness that the Arctic region is both fragile and rich in resources."

Bush's Unilateralism

The text of the directive also contains a suggestion of the unilateralism that has sparked much international criticism of Bush.

"The United States has broad and fundamental national security interests in the Arctic region and is prepared to operate either independently or in conjunction with other states to safeguard these interests," the text says.

"The United States also has fundamental homeland security interests in preventing terrorist attacks and mitigating

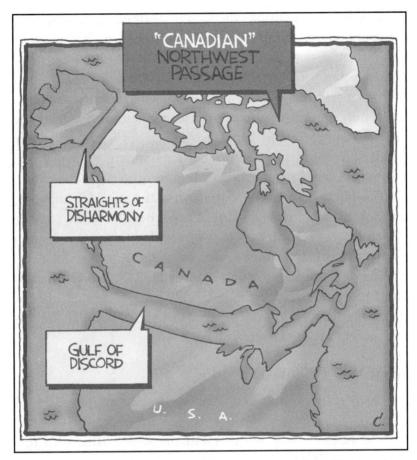

those criminal or hostile acts that could increase the United States' vulnerability to terrorism in the Arctic region.

"This requires the United States to assert a more active and influential national presence to protect its Arctic interests and to project sea power throughout the region."

U.S. Asserts Its Interests in the Region

The document also urges U.S. co-operation in a number of bilateral settings, including the Arctic Council and the International Maritime Organization to develop "new international arrangements" as human activity in the region grows.

The directive instructs the U.S. to aggressively resolve border disputes, particularly in the Arctic seabed, so it can determine where it may lay claim to resources.

"Defining with certainty the area of the Arctic seabed and subsoil in which the United States may exercise its sovereign rights over natural resources such as oil, natural gas, methane hydrates, minerals, and living marine species is critical to our national interests in energy security, resource management, and environmental protection," the directive states.

The policy also notes that Canada and the U.S. "have an unresolved boundary dispute in the Beaufort Sea ... the United States recognizes that the boundary area may contain oil, natural gas, and other resources."

The directive says the best way for the U.S. to win international recognition for its boundary disputes is through the international convention on the Law of the Sea [United Nations Convention on the Law of the Sea].

What Will Obama Do?

Bush's directive is the first U.S. Arctic policy update in 15 years.

It is not yet clear whether Obama would adhere to this policy, dump it or create his own.

However, in the heat of the U.S. presidential race last summer [2008], Obama acknowledged the need to co-operate with Canada on energy issues, saying that completing the Alaska Gas Pipeline with Canada would help ease U.S. dependency on offshore oil.

Energy and environmental issues will feature prominently when Obama arrives in Ottawa in the coming weeks for a meeting with Harper on what will be his first foreign trip as president.

> "Poverty exists because of the choices we
> make. We need to make the right ones."

Canada Should Not Slash Foreign Aid

Gerry Barr

Gerry Barr is the president and chief executive officer of the Canadian Council for International Co-Operation. In the following viewpoint, he argues that by freezing aid spending, the Canadian government has effectively turned its back on the poor. Barr praises recent legislation that ties foreign aid spending to ending poverty while taking into account international human rights standards.

As you read, consider the following questions:

1. According to Barr, how many people are malnourished worldwide?

2. By what percentage does the Canadian government need to increase aid spending annually to meet United Nations' targets for aid spending?

3. With the freeze, Canada will drop to what position out of twenty-two donor countries in terms of generosity?

Gerry Barr, "Shameful Retreat on Foreign Aid," *Toronto Star*, March 13, 2010. Reprinted with permission.

Foreign aid was hit hard in last week's [March 2010] federal budget as Finance Minister Jim Flaherty announced a freeze on aid spending.

It's easy to get lost in numbers, percentages and charts, but in a world where more than 1 billion people are undernourished and 72 million children are unable to go to school, we should never forget that when we talk about foreign aid we're talking about the human struggle to escape poverty and pursue a life of dignity.

What, then, does the federal budget say about Canada's commitment to help end global poverty?

Conservative Government Stiffs the Poor

Significantly, this was the first budget to showcase the Conservative approach to foreign aid spending, as the 8 per cent increases to aid in previous Conservative budgets had made good on a Liberal premise to double aid spending by 2010. But given the opportunity to put its own stamp on Canada's role in the world, the Conservative government chose to turn its back on the world's poor.

In order to meet the United Nations' target for aid spending of 0.7 per cent of gross national income, the government needed to announce 14 per cent annual increases to aid spending for the next 10 years. We needed 14 per cent—we got zero.

With this budget, Canada, in terms of generosity, will fall to the back of the pack—18th out of 22 donor countries for aid, Canada's lowest ranking ever.

This leadership failure is surprising as it comes in a year when the international spotlight will be on Canada. World leaders will meet here in June [2010] for the G8 and G20 summits [Group of 8 and Group of 20, forums for the world's industrialized and developing economies].

Canada Fails to Lead on Aid Issue

More perplexing, this freeze on aid spending comes after the government has announced that maternal and child health will be a priority for the G8 meeting. Last week's budget, in fact, stated that Canada will "work to secure global spending on this priority." Canada can't lead by calling on world leaders to act and then fail to back the call with the monies needed.

In addition to the maternal and child health announcement, Canada has, recently and rightly, committed to double aid to agriculture and to provide long-term support to Haiti as it rebuilds following the devastating earthquake.

But with zero increases to the aid budget, these and other aid programs may suffer as the government will end up having to "rob Peter to pay Paul."

This lack of funding should not be rationalized away because we are in the midst of a global financial crisis. It is the poorest and most vulnerable in developing countries who are suffering most. The financial crisis is driving nearly 50 million more people into extreme poverty as jobs are lost.

Other Countries Honor Their Obligations

Other aid donors have managed to maintain their aid performance despite dealing with more serious impacts on government finances from the global financial crisis than those experienced by Canada.

The United Kingdom is on track to reach the 0.7 per cent target by 2013 and a number of countries—Sweden, Norway, Denmark and the Netherlands—continue to be highly generous, with aid commitments well above the 0.7 per cent target.

In 2010, Canada's contribution will fall to 0.33 per cent and plummet to 0.28 per cent by 2014. Canada's performance is nothing short of an international embarrassment.

But international reputation aside, foreign aid matters. It matters in terms of quantity, but also quality.

On the quality side, Canada recently passed legislation focusing foreign aid spending on ending poverty while taking into account the voices of the poor and international human rights standards.

This legislation matters because it means that aid cannot be politicized to further foreign policy agendas. It matters because it means that foreign aid must be consistent with human rights and integral to the ability of the world's poor to claim their human rights—the right to food, health and education.

On the quantity side, unfortunately, this federal budget is an indication that Canada is not serious about ending global poverty.

Foreign aid matters because poverty is not inevitable. Poverty exists because of the choices we make. We need to make the right ones.

Canada Should Focus Less on Amount of Aid and More on Using It Efficiently

Beverley J. Oda

Beverley J. Oda is the Canadian Minister of International Cooperation. In the following viewpoint excerpted from a speech, she outlines the accomplishments of the Canadian International Development Agency (CIDA) and describes how Canadian foreign aid has helped needy people all over the world. Oda argues that the Canadian aid system is reevaluating the way it allocates foreign aid to more effectively target aid to those who need it most and to where it can make the most difference.

As you read, consider the following questions:

1. In 2008 Oda announced that Canada was increasing its food aid commitment to what amount of money?

Beverley J. Oda, "Speaking Notes by the Honourable Beverley J. Oda on International Cooperation Days," Canadian International Development Agency, November 17, 2008. Reprinted with permission.

2. What does the term "untying aid" mean?

3. How is CIDA changing the way it works on the ground, according to Oda?

Today, more than ever, it is important that we demonstrate to Canadians that their tax dollars are making a measurable contribution to improving the quality of life in developing countries.

This conference is part of an ongoing conversation between long-term partners borne of the shared goal of reducing poverty in challenging times.

This government has made accountability a hallmark of its agenda.

We have also positioned international development assistance as an important part of Canada's foreign policy.

Our government has made firm commitments since taking office in 2006.

Our international assistance envelope continues to grow, in fact, by 2010–11 it will be twice what it was in 2001–02.

This fiscal year, we will meet our G8 [Group of 8, a forum for the world's major industrialized nations] commitment to double Canada's aid to Africa.

Other Commitments

The Prime Minister [Stephen Harper] has also committed to re-engaging the Americas, and as part of that pledge, Canada has made multi-year commitments to Haiti and the Caribbean region.

We have made major commitments to Sudan and the West Bank/Gaza; focusing our efforts on stability, peace and humanitarian support.

And just this year [2008], we made significant commitments to fight AIDs [acquired immune deficiency syndrome], tuberculosis and malaria.

Nowhere is our focus on development results more evident than in Canada's efforts in Afghanistan.

Our first report to Parliament on Canada's engagement in Afghanistan highlights a renewed focus for our engagement with clear priorities for the 2008–11 period.

We announced signature projects that will make a difference in the lives of the Afghan people, to be delivered more efficiently and effectively.

Projects that will be recognized by Afghans and Canadians as Canada's key part of our contribution to rebuilding Afghanistan.

These include:

- Repairing the Dahla Dam and its irrigation system;

- Building, expanding or repairing 50 schools in key districts of Kandahar province; and

- Helping to eradicate polio in Afghanistan by the end of 2009.

And for the first time, we will be reporting on benchmarks to measure our progress.

This new approach to Canada's effort in Afghanistan reflects a broader set of reforms to aid effectiveness and how CIDA [Canadian International Development Agency] will operate in the future.

Budgets 2007 and 2008 set out an agenda for Canada's development assistance programs to make them more focused, more efficient and more accountable.

Criticism of Canada's Aid Program

As Minister of International Cooperation, I have read and heard the criticisms about Canada's aid program.

I have heard that CIDA's programs are too diffuse, the Agency is too headquarters-centric and it is too difficult to assess overall effectiveness.

And I can understand those criticisms.

At a time of economic downturn, it is our responsibility not to abandon the world's most vulnerable but to heighten our responsibility to the effectiveness of our international aid.

More instability and decreased access to these basic needs means loss of hope and aspirations for millions around the world.

We need to rethink our international aid to sharpen even more our international aid effectiveness.

The primary test for aid effectiveness must be striving for real outcomes, real results, making a real difference.

It means enabling self-sufficiency and sustainability by local communities and governments.

Fulfilling Canada's Obligations

And so, today, I want to outline how we will be fulfilling our promise to transform Canada's approach to aid over the next few years.

Our new agenda for aid effectiveness will be focused on results.

And it will help Canadians—the real aid donors—to see how their taxpayer dollars are being spent.

Canadians want to see that our efforts are making a real difference in the lives of people who need our help.

In this first stage, Canada's effectiveness agenda is based on a three-pronged approach:

- Maximizing efficiency;

- Strengthening our geographic focus; and

- Ensuring greater accountability.

First, maximizing efficiency.

Targeting Aid More Efficiently

Every dollar not used as efficiently as possible means less for the millions living in poverty.

It means, for example, fewer children with access to education, clean water and health services.

The traditional practice of donor nations, including Canada, was to require that a portion of aid funds be used to purchase goods and services from the donor country.

That practice could imply that aid is as much about helping ourselves as it is about helping others.

The Organisation for Economic Co-operation and Development estimates that tied aid raises the cost of many goods and services by 15 to 30 per cent—and 35 per cent for food aid.

In April [2008], I announced Canada was increasing its food aid commitment to help address the current food crisis, bringing it to $230 million.

But we didn't just write a cheque and leave it at that.

We also completely untied Canada's food aid policy.

The international community welcomed this move.

At a UN [United Nations] Food Summit in Rome that followed our announcement, Josette Sheeran, the World Food Programme's Executive Director said:

> "I want to thank Canada. Canada was a key contributor and all the money it gave was not tied.... The more flexibility we have, the more lives we can save."

The Practice of Untying Aid

Untying aid means that the necessary food and aid supplies may be purchased at a lower price, reducing transportation time frames and benefiting local producers and suppliers in countries seeking economic growth.

In September, to further the efficiency of Canada's aid dollars, I announced that the Government of Canada will untie ALL of its development aid by 2012–13.

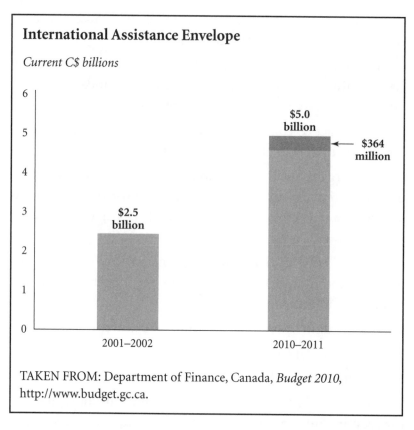

International Assistance Envelope

Current C$ billions

TAKEN FROM: Department of Finance, Canada, *Budget 2010*, http://www.budget.gc.ca.

As highlighted in Budgets 2007 and 2008, our government's commitment to greater aid effectiveness includes reducing administrative overhead and constantly benchmarking ourselves against international best practices.

Secondly, the work of CIDA personnel—like the work of the people and organizations present here today—in the often difficult environments of developing countries should be a source of pride for all Canadians.

CIDA Plans

I would like to take a moment to mention that how CIDA in particular is working on the ground is changing.

In the coming months, we will be increasing our field presence and re-examining our decision-making processes.

This will put more personnel closer to our partners in the field, allowing us to better assess the needs and to develop even more effective responses.

In turn, this will provide for better reporting on results.

This will also allow CIDA to respond more promptly and efficiently to crises and to local environmental, political and humanitarian changes.

This means that Canadian staff will be more visible in the communities where our aid money is making a difference.

And we will delegate more decision making into the field allowing for quicker responses and more informed decisions.

CIDA field staff will have increased financial authority and powers.

While all the necessary audit and accountability measures will remain, this will reduce the burden of redundant head office processing and consequent delays.

Like other donor countries around the world, Canada is also driving toward greater country focus.

Country Focus

The second element of the aid effectiveness agenda, which we will be working on in the next few months, is country focus.

Country focus means achieving the critical mass necessary for our aid to make a stronger and more visible difference.

Dispersing our resources, through a multiplicity of programs in numerous countries, means our efforts have little potential for real impact.

By concentrating our resources, Canada will have greater influence and impact in those countries.

How to Focus Aid Efficiently

The process of focusing our bilateral program will be based on a mix of several key factors.

First, we will look at a country's need, considering national poverty levels and other humanitarian indexes.

Then, we will look at performance measures that rate a country's potential to achieve results effectively.

And finally, we will assess whether Canadian support can make a real difference in that country.

Wherever we have programs, we will seek to work with the governments of these countries to ensure that our efforts are in line with their country's national plans.

The shape of our bilateral program will be developed against the backdrop of Canada's broader foreign policy priorities.

Strengthened alignment between our development program and foreign policy is critical.

Our global, multilateral and regional relationships and investments will remain strong and Canada's humanitarian assistance will continue to be a beacon for those in crisis.

We recently demonstrated this in our rapid response to natural disasters, our significant increase in food aid in the face of the food crisis, and our support to the Global Fund [to Fight] AIDS, Tuberculosis and Malaria, and of the Canadian-led "Initiative to Save a Million Lives."

Accountability

The third aspect of our agenda for aid effectiveness deals with accountability.

Accountability is at the core of all that we do as governments.

In the context of international development, accountability is owed to both our citizens and to those people who live in partner countries—and it is in that spirit that our government supported the Official Development Assistance Accountability Act.

Strengthening public expenditure management systems, and monitoring and evaluation functions must help inform policy making and budget decisions, as well as track progress and the results achieved.

And so, CIDA is working to strengthen the monitoring and evaluation functions of our aid program.

We will measure results by means of a more independent audit function, consistent with the *Federal Accountability Act.*

We will also strengthen the independence of the Agency's evaluation committee.

The majority of members will come from outside CIDA and will include representatives of other federal departments, as well as nongovernment representatives.

This will lead to greater accountability and transparency.

Transparency also means reporting to Canadians on the results achieved with their generosity.

At this conference, we are distributing the first *Canada's International Assistance at Work: Development for Results 2007.*

This new report series aims to bring together development results, presented in plain language, as a snapshot of Canada's aid program.

Transparency and Feedback Are Key

Given that this is our first edition, we would welcome your comments and feedback, as we work to improve our reporting in the coming years.

Canadians will be able to see the results, as we track our progress in clear and measurable ways over time.

And I know that you—CIDA's many partners—are supportive of our efforts towards greater effectiveness and efficiency.

In fact, as recently as the Accra High-Level Forum on Aid Effectiveness in September—thanks to the considerable efforts of Canadian civil society organizations [CSOs]. CSOs became genuine partners in trying to advance aid effectiveness.

For many of you in this room, your tireless commitment to those in poverty around the world is based on a strong belief that all people should be assisted in their move from dependence to self-reliance.

And so, I would like to commend our Canadian NGO [nongovernmental organization] partners for their continued contributions and hard work.

Aid effectiveness, of course, is about more than just commitments and changes made by donor countries—it is also about how we work with our partner countries.

I have seen firsthand how a country can benefit from more focused, effective and accountable development aid.

Making a Difference in Afghanistan and Honduras

During my visits to Afghanistan, I have seen boys and girls learning together in schools.

I have seen women walking freely in the streets of Kabul, enjoying the freedoms that we here in Canada so often take for granted.

And I met a young man at the teacher's college, who in reply to the question "why did he choose to become a teacher?" he answered, "to help rebuild my country."

In Honduras, I saw a water project that is making a real difference in villages in Ramal del Tigre, on the north coast of the country.

The project brought potable water from new water reservoirs straight into people's homes, replacing long treks to the nearest questionable water source.

The entire system is now under the management of a local community water management council and local people have been trained to maintain the system and test the water regularly.

By including the local community in the planning, construction and maintenance of the system, a project that formerly would have included over 40 foreign workers, was completed with about eight NGO staff on site.

This is a fine example of effective and efficient development.

The Hondurans had an undeniable sense of accomplishment and ownership.

The emotion I witnessed as one woman brought me to see her kitchen tap and washtub, both with running water, made me appreciate what making a difference means.

Canada's Support Is Needed

I've seen gratitude for Canada's support in the faces of children in schools in Haiti, mothers receiving nutritious meals at women's centres in Peru, families lined up outside of a health clinic in Tanzania or the men who were building their own irrigation ditches.

These experiences compelled me even more to work with my colleagues to ensure that Canada's aid is the most effective, coherent and efficient aid we as a country could deliver.

At the same time, as part of the international community, we can only go so far on our own to achieve our goals of greater focus and effectiveness.

Clearly, we must work harder to improve the dialogue among all partners to achieve increased accountability, cohesion, co-ordination and focus.

Improving Canada's Aid System

Canada will continue to be a strong advocate for improving our collective efforts.

This was the case in Tokyo at the G8 development minister's meeting, in London at the Ad Hoc Liaison Committee's meeting, or at the annual meeting of the Caribbean Development Bank in Halifax, and in Accra at the High-Level Forum on Aid Effectiveness.

In Accra, more than 1,500 delegates representing bilateral and multilateral donors, partner countries and civil society came together to ensure that momentum on aid effectiveness was maintained.

In addition, when opportunities arise, I reinforce the importance of working with countries to strengthen their abilities to develop sustainable conditions and their capacity to deliver basic services to their populations.

Our agenda for aid effectiveness reflects the values of all Canadians.

And this is another way in which our government is working hard to restore Canada's reputation as a principled leader on the world stage.

We are ready to do our part in the world.

Representing Canada and Its Values

We know that Canada has a time-honoured tradition of helping those less fortunate than ourselves, and in making a difference in the lives of those living in poverty in the world's poorest countries.

And I am proud to be part of a government that is committed to that tradition and to making the help offered as beneficial as possible to the people whose need is the greatest.

We are counting on you to help implement our agenda for aid effectiveness.

It will take all of our efforts, talent and expertise to make a real difference in reducing poverty around the world.

I am confident that, out of these meetings will come the ideas and synergy that will take us one step closer to that reality.

Periodical and Internet Sources Bibliography

The following articles have been selected to supplement the diverse views presented in this chapter.

Mike Blanchfield	"Canada's Foreign Aid to Be More Accountable Not Larger: Minister," *National Post*, May 20, 2009.
Bruce Campion-Smith	"Ottawa Plans an Arctic Thaw," *Toronto Star*, August 21, 2010.
Barry Carin and Gordon Smith	"Unchain Canada's Foreign-Aid Giant," *Globe and Mail*, May 12, 2010.
Rob Gillies	"Competing Claims over Arctic Region," *Washington Post*, August 8, 2007.
John Ibbitson	"Stephen Harper's Northern Renaissance," *Globe and Mail*, August 26, 2010.
Tim Kennelly	"Afghanistan Crisis Deepens: U.S., Canada and NATO Threaten to Extend War," Global Research, August 25, 2010. www.globalresearch.ca.
Eric Morse	"Canada Has to Stand by Its Friends," *Gazette* (Montreal), August 10, 2010.
Vic Neufeld	"Canada's Liberals Press for Extension of Afghan Occupation," World Socialist Web Site, August 11, 2010. www.wsws.org.
Jeffrey Simpson	"Solving Our Problems on the Backs of the Poor," *Globe and Mail*, March 29, 2010.
Paul Wells	"The Arctic: Au nord, peu de nouveau," *Maclean's*, August 20, 2010.
Barbara Yaffe	"Harper Must Not Dilute Sovereignty Message," *Vancouver Sun*, August 21, 2010.

CHAPTER 3

What Challenges to Freedom of Expression Does Canada Face?

Chapter Preface

On October 26, 2006, the Canadian newsweekly *Maclean's* published "The Future Belongs to Islam," an article written by the Canadian author and political commentator Mark Steyn. An excerpt from his best-selling book *America Alone: The End of the World as We Know It*, the article takes a long look at demographic trends in Europe, concluding that Muslims are on track to become the majority population in much of the continent. It also views this trend as a threat to Europe as we know it. "On the Continent and elsewhere in the West, native populations are aging and fading and being supplanted remorselessly by a young Muslim demographic," Steyn states in his article. "Time for the obligatory 'of courses': *of course*, not all Muslims are terrorists—though enough are hot for jihad to provide an impressive support network of mosques from Vienna to Stockholm to Toronto to Seattle. *Of course*, not all Muslims support terrorists.... But, at the very minimum, this fast-moving demographic transformation provides a huge comfort zone for the jihadists to move around in. And in a more profound way it rationalizes what would otherwise be the nuttiness of the terrorists' demands."

In 2007 a group of Muslim law students filed a complaint with the Ontario Human Rights Commission, charging that *Maclean's* refusal to provide them an opportunity to rebut the points made in the article violated their human rights. They then cited twenty-two more *Maclean's* articles, many of them also written by Steyn, that were derogatory toward Muslims and promoted hatred against them as a minority group. Complaints were also filed with the Canadian Human Rights Commission and the British Columbia Human Rights Tribunal.

Human rights tribunals and commissions in Canada have become a lightning rod for controversy. When first established in 1977, the Canadian Human Rights Commission (CHRC) was tasked with investigating and adjudicating complaints of employment discrimination and housing. However, section 13 of the 1977 Canadian Human Rights Act authorized the CHRC to hear complaints about material "likely to expose a person or persons to hatred or contempt" by reason of race, age, gender, disability, marital status, sexual orientation, religion, etc. As the years passed, the CHRC used that clause to regulate and place limits on hate speech—such as what was charged against Steyn and *Maclean's*.

In April 2008 the Ontario Human Rights Commission rejected the complaint, stating it lacked jurisdiction to deal with magazine content. It did issue a statement condemning Steyn and the magazine for a biased, Islamophobic depiction of Muslim people. Critics of the commission were shocked by the statement, arguing that Steyn and *Maclean's* were pronounced guilty without a fair hearing.

A few months later, the CHRC weighed in, dismissing the complaint against *Maclean's* because the views expressed in Steyn's article were not extreme under the existing law. It did, however, note that the article was meant to be provocative and offensive to some readers.

The Steyn incident is a key controversy in the debate over the role of the CHRC, which is central to the following chapter on the major challenges faced by Canada on the issue of free speech. Other viewpoints in the chapter debate Canada's cultural nationalist policies and Quebec's divisive attempt to ban the niqab, a veil that covers the hair and face except for the eyes of a Muslim woman.

| "The right to not be offended trumps
| freedom of speech in Alberta."

Canada's Human Rights Commissions Infringe on Free Speech

Ezra Levant

Ezra Levant is an author, political commentator, and publisher of the Western Standard, *a conservative Canadian newsmagazine. In the following viewpoint, Levant describes his difficult and costly encounter with Canada's human rights commissions (HRCs), which he suggests have been "hijacked as weapons against speech that offends members of minority groups." Levant underlines his defense of free speech as integral to defending Canadian values against encroaching political correctness backed by the power of the state.*

As you read, consider the following questions:

1. When were the controversial cartoons published in Levant's *Western Standard?*

2. What did Syed Soharwardy call Levant for publishing the controversial cartoons?

Ezra Levant, "The Internet Saved My Tongue," *Reason*, June 2009. Reprinted with permission.

3. What would be the penalties if Levant had refused to be interrogated by the Alberta Human Rights and Citizenship Commission?

Early on the morning of February 13, 2006, nearly 40,000 copies of the *Western Standard* rolled off the presses in Edmonton, Alberta. Tucked inside that week's issue of Canada's only national conservative magazine, on pages 15 and 16, was a story about the international controversy over a Danish newspaper that had printed a dozen satirical cartoons featuring the prophet Muhammad [founder of Islam]. Our article, which was illustrated by eight of the cartoons, would soon trigger a three-year government investigation of whether I, as the *Western Standard*'s publisher, had violated the rights of Canadian Muslims by "discriminating" against their religion.

The investigation vividly illustrated how Canada's provincial and national human rights commissions (HRCs), created in the 1970s to police discrimination in employment, housing, and the provision of goods and services, have been hijacked as weapons against speech that offends members of minority groups. My eventual victory over this censorious assault suggests that Western governments will find it increasingly difficult in the age of the Internet to continue undermining human rights in the name of defending them.

Background of the Cartoons in Question

By commissioning the Muhammad cartoons, the Danish newspaper, the *Jyllands-Posten*, was making a point about the West's fear of insulting Islam. A Danish author and longtime leftist activist named Kåre Bluitgen had written a children's book about Muhammad, but because some Muslims consider visual depictions of their prophet taboo, Bluitgen found it difficult to find an illustrator. *Jyllands-Posten* editors wanted to highlight this Danish culture of self-censorship and show the newspaper's support for freedom of speech by publishing their own cartoons of Muhammad.

A few of the images were critical of radical Islam, but the criticism wasn't any harsher than that routinely heaped on other religions and ideologies in the editorial cartoons of Western newspapers. One showed Muhammad in heaven, saying, "Stop, stop, we ran out of virgins!" as suicide bombers floated up to the clouds. Another depicted Muhammad wearing a turban in the shape of a bomb.

The cartoons were published in September 2005, but they didn't make international news until the next year, when a group of Danish imams [Muslim leaders] went on a world tour to drum up Muslim anger against Denmark. The imams brought three additional cartoons along with the original dozen. Those three additions, which hadn't been published in Denmark or anywhere else, were grotesque, including one showing Muhammad having sex with a dog. They were the imams' own handiwork, added to the bundle in case the *Jyllands-Posten* efforts didn't achieve the desired response. Up until that moment, the phrase cartoon violence had summoned to mind images no more harmful than Wile E. Coyote fighting the Road Runner. But after the imam tour in the spring of 2006, more than 100 people died in purportedly spontaneous riots against the cartoons. Half a dozen terrorist plots to avenge the artwork were uncovered across Europe. Demagogic governments from Tehran to Damascus seized the opportunity to deflect attention away from their own problems.

Every newspaper and TV station in the Western world covered the story of the riots, but almost none of them showed the original cartoons themselves. The media's self-censorship was based on the same fear exhibited by Denmark's illustrators. As a journalist, I was appalled by this cowardice masquerading as sensitivity. *Western Standard* editor Kevin Libin and I knew our readers would be interested in this story and would want to see for themselves what all the fuss was about.

Making National News

As our publication date drew nearer, we couldn't help noticing that no other mainstream publication in Canada was planning to reprint the cartoons. We'd be the first, and possibly only, one. We sent the magazine to our printers on Friday, February 10, for printing over the weekend. The next day, word of the deed somehow leaked. By Sunday our decision had become national news, even though no one except our staff and our printers had seen the spread.

I must have done 100 interviews that week. The first would be particularly memorable. At 7 a.m. on Monday, February 13, while our magazine was being trucked from our printers to the post office, I appeared on the Canadian Broadcasting Corporation's [CBC's] *Eyeopener* radio show in Calgary. The amiable Jim Brown was the host, and the other guest was Syed Soharwardy. All I knew about Soharwardy at the time was that he was a Pakistani immigrant to Canada who worked for IBM and had a part-time gig as a preacher at a tiny mosque in a northeast Calgary strip mall. Soharwardy had very few followers—about 40 congregants in a city that was home to thousands of Muslims. But he was a big-time media hound, always trolling for interviews while the city's more prominent imams rolled their eyes.

I explained the newsworthiness of the cartoons. But Soharwardy wasn't quite in sync with our Canadian concepts of freedom of the press and the separation of religion and state. He called me a "terrorist" for publishing the cartoons—a bit rich, coming from someone who, I later learned, does the radical Muslim lecture circuit in Saudi Arabia. Then he announced to startled CBC listeners that he was a direct descendant of Muhammad and therefore felt personally offended. I wasn't quite sure what to do with that one, so I kept on message, saying Soharwardy was free to follow the Koran [the main religious text of Islam] as his law, but we were in Canada, not Saudi Arabia. People like me could publish whatever they liked. The debate degenerated into a shouting match.

Complaints Are Filed

With other interviews to get to, I soon put the verbal fracas out of mind. Soharwardy did not. He was accustomed to fawning media treatment, bestowed by politically correct reporters delighted to have a spot of diversity in their news. He wasn't used to facing disagreement or being called a radical. In Pakistan, where Soharwardy had been a student at a madrassah [a Muslim school that is part of a mosque], someone who spoke that way to the imams would have been whipped. In Saudi Arabia, where Soharwardy had lectured at an officially anti-Semitic university, my blasphemy might even have resulted in the loss of my head.

So Soharwardy visited the Calgary Police Service, where he demanded that I be arrested. The police politely explained to him that he wasn't in Saudi Arabia or Pakistan anymore and that police in Canada don't enforce the Koran or get involved in political disputes. Next he filed a complaint with the Alberta Human Rights and Citizenship Commission (AHRCC). This body was more receptive to the idea that I should be punished for giving offense.

The AHRCC sent me a copy of Soharwardy's complaint, a mishmash of personal braggadocio, Islamic supremacism, and whining, all handwritten in English surprisingly broken for someone who had been living in Canada for 20 years. It was riddled with misspellings, including erroneous renditions of my name and the name of my magazine. But the nature of Soharwardy's thinking still managed to shine through.

Questionable Claims

"Ezra Lavant [sic] insulted me on air on CBC radio," Soharwardy wrote. "He also said that the hateful cartoons are justified to be published in his magazine *Western Standards.*" He complained that "CBC, CTV and other media" dared to speak with me. Noting that he was "openly the follower and related to Prophet Muhammad," Soharwardy wrote that our publication of the cartoons "have sighted violence, hate and discrimination against my family and me." Such incitement (I'm guessing that's what he meant) would have been quite a feat, given that the magazines hadn't yet landed in any mailboxes and wouldn't be on newsstands for another week.

As proof of his claims, Soharwardy included a raft of e-mail messages he had received, including one that called him "excitable" and "humourless" and told him to "laugh" a little more. Another message said that there "are many fine Muslims out there," but that radical Islam deserved to be mocked. This was the "violence" that Soharwardy faced: ordinary Canadians telling him off.

Soharwardy followed up his original complaint with a detailed list of legal arguments—but not from any Canadian law books. He cited passages from the Koran as his precedent, insisting that "the respect and obedience to Prophet Muhammad is the most basic requirement of Faith." At the end of his letter, he offered both artistic and religious criticism of all eight of our Muhammad images, adding, "I am quite disturbed and mentally tortured by these cartoons." And his demands were clear: "I am expecting a formal apology . . . from the *Western Standard*. Please help."

The AHRCC Gets Involved

The AHRCC [Alberta Human Rights and Citizenship Commission] was more than happy to help. The Alberta Human Rights, Citizenship, and Multiculturalism Act prohibits publishing anything that "is likely to expose a person or class of persons to hatred or contempt." The theory was that hurtful words necessarily lead to hurtful deeds, and the vagueness of the law meant it was particularly useful as a tool of political censorship.

I consulted Tom Ross, a Calgary lawyer experienced in dealing with HRC complaints. Ross said there were two ways to respond: We could try to make the problem go away quickly, possibly with a cash payment, an apology, and participation in a re-education session. Or we could fight like hell. After that initial conversation, we didn't waste any time talking about option number one. I was outraged that a government agency was getting involved with the editorial decisions of our magazine.

The *Western Standard* was prepared to debate our decision to run the cartoons, but voluntarily, in a process involving our subscribers (who enthusiastically agreed with our decision), our advertisers (who were nervous at first but ultimately supported us), and our distributors (most of whom stood with us and saw strong newsstand sales). In the edition following the one in which the cartoons appeared, we ran an extended letters section, with the entire spectrum of views represented, including a worried mother of a Canadian soldier in Afghanistan, a Muslim immigrant to Canada who said she wanted to get away from Shariah law, and nutcases who said I published the cartoons only because I was Jewish. That's what a public debate in Canada looks like.

A Defense of Free Speech

Soharwardy didn't participate. He preferred a Shariah-style solution. Six weeks after we published the cartoons, when members of the public had already chewed the issues over and made up their minds, when the commotion was dying down and we decided to let our extra security staff go, I got around to writing the *Western Standard*'s reply to Soharwardy's complaint. "The complaint is a frivolous and vexatious abuse of process," I began. "It has no basis in fact or Canadian law. It is contrary to Canadian values of freedom of speech, freedom of the press and religious plurality, under which Canadians are free from compulsion to submit to religious edicts. The complaint is an attempt to abuse the power of the state to chill discussion about subjects that are in the public interest. It is also an inappropriate combination of mosque and state, using a secular government agency to enforce a Muslim religious precept, namely the fundamentalist prohibition of the depiction of Mohammed."

I still believe every word of that, but it's a bit embarrassing that I actually thought those principles mattered. As I learned since, the right to not be offended trumps freedom of speech in Alberta. That's the official position of the provincial government, as argued by its lawyer in *Lund v. Boissoin*, a case in which a Christian pastor was given a lifetime ban prohibiting him from criticizing gay marriage.

"If the [Commission] does not dismiss this complaint," I continued, "the AHRCC will be discredited and its liberal reputation will be brought into disrepute. This complaint perverts the cause of human rights. If the AHRCC allows itself to be used to attack the publication of a good faith debate on these issues, the AHRCC will become a tool of censorship. . . . The AHRCC will send a message that the state, with its unlimited resources, will not hesitate to interfere with and harass media that discuss controversial topics."

A Tool for Censorship

Unfortunately, I got that part right. A year later, in March 2007, *Maclean's* magazine was hauled before three human rights commissions to answer for its discussion of radical Islam, in the form of an excerpt from Mark Steyn's best-selling book, *America Alone: The End of the World as We Know It*. Two years later, the Alberta commission ruled that Rev. Stephen Boissoin, a Christian pastor from Red Deer, may never again preach against gay marriage—or even disparage it in private e-mails. Needless to say, such gag orders cast a pall over public discussions of these issues.

I also had a sense that fighting the complaint would be costly. "Even an acquittal ... is a punishment," I wrote. "The process becomes the penalty." I had no idea, however, that the process would stretch on for three years and cost me more than $100,000. The trouble and expense of such investigations help explain why so many people roll over when faced with a human rights complaint.

Eight months passed.

The AHRCC offered to set up a "conciliation meeting" with Soharwardy and representatives from the Edmonton Council of Muslim Communities, which had filed an almost identical complaint. I told the commission there could be only one form of "conciliation" that I would accept: that these complainants reconcile themselves to Canadian values and leave their Saudi-style approach to free speech overseas. The AHRCC's next move was to offer me a plea bargain: It told Tom Ross, my lawyer, that if I agreed to publish an apology in the magazine and pay a few thousand dollars to the complainants, I could walk free. I replied that I would fight the AHRCC and its hijackers all the way to the Canadian Supreme Court before I did that—and even if I lost there, I'd contemplate doing jail time for contempt of court before apologizing.

The Next Step

One year after I had rejected the commission's terms of surrender, it told Ross it was launching a formal investigation. I was to present myself to a "human rights officer" to be interrogated about my decision to print the controversial cartoons. If I refused the AHRCC's "invitation" to be interrogated, its officers, under Section 23 of the Alberta Human Rights, Citizenship, and Multiculturalism Act, could enter my office and seize any "records and documents, including electronic records and documents, that are or may be relevant to the subject matter of the investigation." Computer hard drives, confidential files, private correspondence, even letters between me and

HRCs Are Unjust

As I began to read the facts of [Ezra] Levant's case, I came to the sad realization that Canada no longer has freedom of speech. The "human rights" commissions (HRCs) all over Canada, staffed by bureaucrats and not following normal legal procedures, had originally been set up to deal with blatant cases of discrimination; they had morphed into star chambers weighing in on what the press could print, what pastors could say from the pulpit, whether certain Bible verses could be displayed publicly and so on.

Mark Hemingway, "Northern Discomfort,"
National Review, *April 15, 2009.*

my lawyer could be seized, all without a search warrant. Section 24 of the act allowed AHRCC employees to ask a judge for permission to enter my home and take whatever they liked there, too.

After weeks of haggling over the details, the interrogation was scheduled for Friday, January 11, 2008, nearly two years after we published the cartoons, at my lawyer's office in downtown Calgary. The human rights officer in charge of the investigation—Shirlene McGovern, a bland, middle-aged woman in casual clothes—did not seem intimidating. She arrived smiling and chatty, extending her hand to shake mine. I declined. Then McGovern, who had barred members of the press from the meeting, spotted the video camera we had set up, and she hesitated. She had agreed that I could record the proceedings but hadn't explicitly consented to videotaping. With a shrug, she agreed to the camera. It was a decision she would come to regret.

Levant's Statement

I had prepared an opening statement. "When the *Western Standard* magazine printed the Danish cartoons of Muhammad two years ago," I said, "it was the proudest moment of my public life. I would do it again today. In fact, I did do it again today. . . . I posted the cartoons this morning on my website, EzraLevant.com." It was more refined than telling McGovern to f--- off, but it had the same effect. She was stunned.

"I am here at this government interrogation under protest," I continued. "It is my position that the government has no legal or moral authority to interrogate me or anyone else for publishing these words and pictures. That is a violation of my ancient and inalienable freedoms: freedom of speech, freedom of the press, and in this case, religious freedom and the separation of mosque and state. It is especially perverted that a bureaucracy calling itself the Alberta Human Rights Commission would be the government agency violating my human rights. So I will now call those bureaucrats 'the commission' or 'the HRC,' since to call the commission a 'human rights commission' is to destroy the meaning of those words."

McGovern rolled her eyes. But I kept going. I declared that "the commission is a joke," comparing it unfavorably with Judge Judy. I quoted Alan Borovoy, general counsel of the Canadian Civil Liberties [Association], who had recently condemned the complaints against me as abusive. I called the AHRCC a violation of 800 years of British common law and 250 years of Canadian law, including our 1960 Bill of Rights and our Charter of Rights and Freedoms. I even quoted from the 1948 United Nations Universal Declaration of Human Rights, which protects free speech. "I have no faith in this farcical commission," I concluded. "But I do have faith in the justice and good sense of my fellow Albertans and Canadians. I believe that the better they understand this case, the more shocked they will be."

The Point of Free Speech

At the beginning of her interrogation, McGovern said, "I always ask people . . . what was your intent and purpose of your article?" Always? Just how often does McGovern haul people in for questioning about their politics? That's one of the mysteries about these star chambers; we know only about the cases in which the targets are stubborn enough to fight. According to the HRC's annual reports, the vast majority settle without a hearing. And why did my "purpose and intent" matter? Would the article we ran be legal if I had happy thoughts, but illegal if my thoughts somehow offended the commission's sensibilities?

Toward the end of the meeting, McGovern cavalierly stated, "You're entitled to your opinions, that's for sure." But that just wasn't true, was it? If I had been entitled to my opinions, I wouldn't have been summoned to a 90-minute interrogation by the government on pain of having my office and home searched if I refused. And I wouldn't be standing accused in a human rights proceeding that could end with me being forced to pay tens of thousands of dollars, issue an apology, undergo re-education, and/or refrain from unapproved speech in the future.

| "*Canadians expect fairness and effi-
ciency from their human rights system,
and we must continue to offer both.*"

Canada's Human Rights Commissions Are Vital to Protecting Free Speech

Jennifer Lynch

Jennifer Lynch is chief commissioner of the Canadian Human Rights Commission. In the following viewpoint, she underscores the value of Canada's human rights commissions (HRCs), which she believes balances the right of free expression and the protection of individuals from hate speech. Lynch argues that opponents of HRCs aim to weaken the country's human rights system.

As you read, consider the following questions:

1. What is section 13 of the Canadian Human Rights Act?

2. Why do many people oppose section 13?

3. According to Lynch, who is responsible for ensuring the promotion and protection of human rights?

Jennifer Lynch, "Hate Speech: This Debate Is Out of Balance," *Globe and Mail*, June 12, 2009. Reprinted with permission.

Yesterday [June 11, 2009], the Canadian Human Rights Commission tabled a rare special report to Parliament, the culmination of months of consultation and study on the issue of hate speech on the Internet. Over the course of many months, Canadians have heard arguments that Section 13 of the Canadian Human Rights Act, governing hate on the Internet, serves as a curtailment on freedom of expression.

Section 13 prohibits the repeated electronic transmission of messages that are likely to expose an individual or a group of individuals to hatred or contempt.

Controversy over Attempts to Curb Hate Speech

It has always been a controversial section. A particularly vigorous debate has arisen since 2007, when a complaint (subsequently dismissed) against *Maclean's* magazine was filed. Our report, while proposing amendments to the act, rejects the notion that human rights legislation, and the processes used to enforce it, is an unreasonable restraint on freedom of expression. Support for this view was articulated by the Supreme Court of Canada, which concluded in a 1990 decision that hate propaganda presents a serious threat to society:

> It undermines the dignity and self-worth of target group members and, more generally, contributes to disharmonious relations among various racial, cultural and religious groups, as a result eroding the tolerance and open-mindedness that must flourish in a multicultural society which is committed to the idea of equality.

Tolerance and open-mindedness are ideals to which Canadians have subscribed, and are part of the quest for equality that has come to define our country all over the world. They are the foundation of the Canadian Human Rights Act, whose promise is to give effect "to the principle that all individuals

Advancing the Human Rights System

The Canadian Charter of Rights and Freedoms guarantees all Canadians the right to freedom of expression. The Charter also guarantees all Canadians the right to equality. Extreme hateful expression places these two rights in conflict. Recognizing that no right is absolute, legislators have developed laws and courts have developed jurisprudence that gives guidance in balancing these rights.

Canada's current approach to regulating hate messages—and achieving the necessary balance—involves two avenues of law: the Criminal Code and section 13 of the Canadian Human Rights Act. The two laws address the issue of hateful expression in different ways. The Criminal Code seeks to punish the offender, while the Canadian Human Rights Act seeks to remove hateful messages.

Recently, many Canadians have been engaged in a passionate debate that questions Canada's current mechanisms for preventing hate messages. The Commission's role and its mandate in section 13 of the Canadian Human Rights Act have been at the centre of this discussion.

Canadian Human Rights Commission, Annual Report, 2009.

should have an opportunity equal with other individuals to make for themselves the lives that they are able and wish to have" without discrimination.

Finding a Balance

Some who disagree with this notion would have Canada weaken its human rights system, taking the view that freedom of expression is the paramount right in Canadian society, over and above the right of all citizens to be protected from the harm that can be caused by hate messages.

In fact, there is no hierarchy of rights with some rights having greater importance than others. They work together toward a common purpose.

It is up to legislators and courts to find the appropriate balance that best protects the human rights and freedoms of all citizens. Canada has an enviable track record in this regard, and our Charter of Rights and Freedoms is viewed as a model for other free societies to emulate. Human rights commissions and tribunals provide access to the justice system and remedies for those who believe they are the victims of discrimination. As is the case with all administrative law bodies, they ensure that all parties are protected by the rules of natural justice, and that frivolous complaints are efficiently disposed.

Canadians expect fairness and efficiency from their human rights system, and we must continue to offer both.

The True Agenda of Opponents

However, I believe critics of human rights commissions and tribunals are manipulating information and activities around rights cases and freedom of expression to further a new agenda. This agenda posits that rights commissions and tribunals, and the attendant vigilance over all the rights and freedoms Canadians now enjoy, no longer serve a useful purpose. In this way, the debate over freedom of expression has been used as a wedge to undermine and distort our human rights system.

Ironically, a debate about balancing rights has not itself been balanced. One can only surmise that if these critics succeed, thus would begin a broader assault on freedoms they would subordinate to absolute freedom of expression.

Ensuring the promotion and protection of human rights is a responsibility that belongs to all of us. Our diverse and inclusive society was created through a commitment to equality, dignity and rights. We have come a long way, but we cannot afford to relax our vigilance or declare victory. Together, we must ensure that those who are the most vulnerable in our society are not further marginalized.

To be sure, the debate over freedom of expression and hate messages will continue. The commission welcomes that debate; it is a positive and democratic exercise. By presenting its special report, the commission's aim is to contribute a balanced analysis for those interested in developing informed opinions on this passionate topic.

> "There is nothing that prevents the Government of Canada or the provincial/ territorial governments from reforming their human rights commissions."

Canada's Human Rights Commissions Must Be Reformed

Aaron Goldstein

Aaron Goldstein is a contributor to the Intellectual Conservative website. In the following viewpoint, he discusses the controversy over Canada's human rights commissions (HRCs) and argues that they should be reformed, not abolished. Goldstein maintains that those conservatives questioning the legitimacy of the HRCs should be focusing their efforts on reforming them.

As you read, consider the following questions:

1. Why did Mohamed Elmasry file a complaint against author Mark Steyn and *Maclean's*?

2. When was the Canadian Human Rights Commission established?

Aaron Goldstein, "Is Abolishing Canada's Human Rights Commissions Necessary?" IntellectualConservative.com, December 30, 2007. Reprinted with permission.

3. How did British Columbia reform its human rights system?

Mark Steyn possesses a mighty pen. He writes about the grimmest of subjects, namely the dangers of Islamic fundamentalism. Yet he does so with a wit sharp enough that one nearly forgets what he writes about is no laughing matter. One of my favorite lines in Steyn's 2006 book *America Alone[: The End of the World as We Know It]* was how the membership of the Khartoum Feminist Publishing Collective has grown to the point that "they've rented lavish new offices above the clitorectomy clinic." Naturally, when one is that deliberately provocative there will be those who are less than amused. Needless to say, Islamic fundamentalists are not known for their sense of humor.

Mohamed Elmasry, president of the Canadian Islamic Congress (CIC), has drawn a sword to Steyn's pen by filing complaints with the Canadian Human Rights Commission, as well as provincial human rights tribunals in Ontario and British Columbia. To be exact, Elmasry filed a complaint against both Steyn and *Maclean's* magazine (which is roughly the Canadian equivalent of *Time* or *Newsweek*) for publishing an excerpt from *America Alone* in October 2006. The CIC also wanted to publish an article rebutting Steyn but *Maclean's* editor Kenneth Whyte refused when the CIC demanded he cede editorial control over the article and accompanying artwork. Elmasry argues that both Steyn's article and *Maclean's* decision to publish it constitutes religious discrimination against Muslims. According to Elmasry, in his complaint to the British Columbia Human Rights Tribunal, "Under the British Columbia Human Rights Code, publication of material . . . is prohibited and clearly exceeds the scope of free speech." As of this writing [December 2007], the Canadian and British Columbia tribunals are planning to hear Elmasry's complaint while the Ontario Human Rights Commission has not made a decision in this regard.

Targeting the HRCs

Yet much of the criticism of Canadian conservatives is directed at the human rights commissions rather than Elmasry and the Canadian Islamic Congress. David Warren, a conservative columnist for the *Ottawa Citizen*, describes human rights commissions as "kangaroo courts." In an article that appeared on *National Review Online* on December 11, 2007, Rebecca Walberg, a policy analyst for the Frontier Center for Public Policy, wrote that human rights commissions were little more than "forums for nuisance suits." But are human rights commissions really to blame for the situation in which Mark Steyn and *Maclean's* now find themselves?

For those unfamiliar with the function human rights commissions serve in Canada, here is a brief overview. Human rights legislation prohibiting discrimination in areas such as housing and employment on the basis of race, religion and creed was passed in provinces such as Ontario and Saskatchewan as early as the mid-1940s. However, there was no formal mechanism by which to resolve such complaints when they arose. That is until 1961, when Ontario's Progressive Conservative government of Leslie Frost enacted the Ontario Human Rights Code which was enforced by the first human rights commission in Canada. By the mid-1970s, all the other Canadian provinces and territories had followed suit. The Canadian Human Rights Commission was established in 1977 to address discrimination where it arose in areas of federal jurisdiction.

However, in more recent years, human rights commissions have been criticized for behaving as enforcers of politically correct thought. For instance, in November 2005, the B.C. [British Columbia] Human Rights Tribunal ordered the Knights of Columbus to pay a same-sex lesbian couple damages for refusing to rent them a hall for their wedding. This despite the fact the Knights had voluntarily returned the couple's deposit, bore the cost of renting them a new hall and even reprinted their wedding invitations.

Don't Abolish HRCs

Despite this and some other dubious decisions, I am not convinced the abolition of human rights commissions in Canada is the proper way to address the situation now faced by Mark Steyn and *Maclean's*. I have arrived at this conclusion for three reasons.

First, the abolition of human rights commissions in Canada would not have prevented Elmasry and the CIC from lodging their complaints. If Canada's Parliament and all provincial/territorial legislatures simultaneously voted to abolish their human rights bodies tomorrow, it would not prevent Elmasry from taking action against Steyn and *Maclean's*. Elmasry would simply have taken them to court. Now, it is true there are certain advantages in Elmasry taking the route of the human rights commission. The burden of proof in front of a human rights commission is of a far lower standard than in a court of law. Unlike going to court, when one files a complaint with a human rights commission, the taxpayers pick up the tab. Conversely, Steyn and *Maclean's* must pay for their legal representation. Yet if one goes about and abolishes the human rights commission, these cases, whatever their merit, would instead be filed in the court system and surprise, surprise the court system would have an even larger backlog than it does now. In other words, abolishing the human rights commissions would only shift the problem to another venue. Not only would the absence of human rights commissions in Canada not prevent Elmasry and the CIC . . . from accusing Steyn and *Maclean's* of religious discrimination against Muslims, it would also deny Canadians who have legitimate grievances a forum in which they can be addressed.

Reform, Not Abolish

Second, there is nothing that prevents the Government of Canada or the provincial/territorial governments from reforming their human rights commissions. Of course, this is much easier said than done. Naturally, these commissions have an arm's length relationship with the governments that created them. After all, many of the complaints brought before these commissions are complaints against the governments themselves. So there must be some distance between governments and human rights bodies. It is also worth noting that governments themselves like having this space as well. After all, when a human rights body makes an unpopular decision and an opposition member of the legislature takes a government minister to task about it during question period, all the government minister need do is remind the opposition member the human rights commission is an arm's length agency and that the government is not directly responsible for its decisions. Of course, if a government sets about to make significant changes to a human rights commission, it will inevitably draw fire from certain constituencies which might take it upon themselves to accuse the government of discrimination and insensitivity to minorities and possibly worse. Most governments are reluctant to start such a fight. Yet there are precedents.

Let's look at British Columbia, which is one of the jurisdictions where Elmasry filed his complaint. In 2002, the B.C. Liberal government of Gordon Campbell actually abolished the B.C. Human Rights Commission. (The B.C. Liberal Party is only liberal in name and is actually quite conservative. The conservative banner was picked up by the B.C. Liberals after the collapse of the Social Credit Party in the 1991 provincial election.) All complaints of discrimination are now filed directly with the B.C. Human Rights Tribunal. Previously, complainants could receive assistance directly from the commission in preparing their complaints. Now that responsibility has fallen directly to the complainant. While complainants can seek assistance from the B.C. Human Rights Coalition, a non-profit organization which receives funding from the provincial government, the coalition does not have resources the B.C.

Human Rights Commission once possessed. Whereas the B.C. Human Rights Commission was involved in conducting investigations, preparing reports, public education and monitoring government policy, the Human Rights Tribunal only hears and renders decisions on cases brought before them.

This, of course, does not guarantee the B.C. Human Rights Tribunal will make a decision favorable to Steyn and *Maclean's*. But it does demonstrate that human rights legislation is not written in stone and that some governments are willing to make changes. Given that the current provincial government in B.C. has demonstrated its willingness to change human rights legislation in the past, it is possible this same government could make more changes if the tribunal renders a decision that is contrary to the principle of free speech or to the proper intentions of British Columbia's Human Rights Code.

Role of Partisan Politics

Third, one must also consider that individuals and organizations with conservative political inclinations are also using human rights commissions to their benefit. Again, let us direct our focus on B.C. Two pro-life campus groups have been denied club status at B.C. postsecondary institutions by their respective student unions. One group is at the University of British Columbia [UBC]-Okanagan in Kelowna and the other group is at Capilano College in North Vancouver. (A similar incident took place in Ontario a year ago at Carleton University, my alma mater.) The student union at UBC-Okanagan and Capilano College are both affiliated with the Canadian Federation of Students (CFS), the country's largest student organization. The CFS is an explicitly pro-choice organization and on these grounds their affiliates at UBC-Okanagan and Capilano College denied the pro-life student groups club status. Both groups have filed complaints with the B.C. Human Rights Tribunal against their respective student unions on religious grounds, and the tribunal has agreed to hear both cases. The UBC-Okanagan case will be heard by the tribunal from February 18–21, 2008. [The B.C. Human Rights Tribunal later dismissed the complaint.] A date has not been set concerning the Capilano College case. [Capilano's pro-life group was granted campus club status by the tribunal in 2008.] It is worth noting that the Capilano College club has received assistance from the B.C. Civil Liberties Association. Could you imagine the ACLU [American Civil Liberties Union] providing assistance to a pro-life campus group? So, if the B.C. Civil Liberties Association can help out, then why not Canadian conservatives? In my view, Canadian conservatives would be better served by supporting the political and religious rights of these pro-life student groups in B.C. rather than calling for the elimination of human rights commissions altogether.

So where does this leave Mark Steyn and *Maclean's*? There is no question that Elmasry and the CIC are trying to silence those who would criticize Islamic fundamentalism. A ruling in favor of Elmasry by any of the tribunals in question could severely constrain public debate and those who disseminate it. But by focusing on the legitimacy of human rights commissions, Canadian conservatives are directing their contempt to the court rather than to the court jester. To read Ezra Levant's recent article in the *National Post* and Stanley Kurtz in *The Corner* on *National Review Online*, it appears to be a foregone conclusion that Steyn and *Maclean's* will not prevail. Yet for all the faults of the human rights commissions, I am not prepared to say that the fix is in. Steyn and *Maclean's* should let the process take its course, make their best appeal to reason and let the chips fall where they may.

> "Respecting the need for diversity and competition, nationalist policies are a sustainable and desirable means to achieve the continued growth of Canada's unique, diverse, and vibrant culture."

Canada Should Maintain Fair Cultural Nationalist Policies

P.J. Worsfold

P.J. Worsfold is the cofounder of Crux Strategies and Media. In the following viewpoint, he asserts that Canada should continue its cultural nationalist policies, especially in broadcasting, in order to facilitate the development and strength of a vibrant and diverse national cultural landscape. Worsfold argues that such policies should be carefully monitored to ensure they do not become protectionist in nature.

As you read, consider the following questions:

1. According to the author, how does the free market run counter to the requirements of optimum cultural development?

P.J. Worsfold, "Canada: Policies of Cultural Protectionism and Nationalism," Crux Strategies and Media, March 31, 2007. Reprinted with permission.

2. What two forms can government intervention into cultural affairs take?

3. When were content restrictions in Canadian broadcasting first introduced?

After studying the history of Canadian broadcasting and the volumes of policy debate that have followed, I have arrived at two conclusions. First, cultural diversity and plurality are vital to a nation's well-being. Secondly, cultural activities cannot be sustained by the free market alone.

Cultural Nationalism Makes Sense

Based on these conclusions and the fact that the broadcasting environment is only going to be more technologically advanced and more globally integrated as time passes, it is my contention that it is both possible and desirable for the bodies that govern Canadian broadcasting to sustain polices of cultural nationalism. If properly drafted and implemented, such policies will help facilitate industrial and cultural objectives both locally and globally. However, as with any act of government intervention into the public sphere, once in place, nationalist broadcasting policies must be closely scrutinized. When facilitation moves to control, nationalist policies quickly become protectionist policies, which although always possible, are never desirable or completely effective. While government restrictions on cultural flow may have the country's best interests at heart, their effects on indigenous cultural production and consumption are questionable. Moreover, the intent of such restrictions runs counter to both the evolution of a vibrant and diverse national cultural landscape and the spirit of equitable global trade.

Stemming from the arguments presented above and with reference to a selection of influential government policies and cultural developments from the 1950s onward, this [viewpoint] will explore the feasibility and the desirability of both policy-driven protectionism and nationalism in more detail. As with many issues that relate to culture and national identity, the debate on broadcast policy is replete with confusion over matters of semantics and connotations. In an effort to relieve this confusion and outline the need for government intervention into the cultural sphere, I will begin by outlining the key definitions and assumptions that my argument hinges on. Next, I will introduce the concepts of cultural protectionism and cultural nationalism and discuss how government policy can implement these concepts. Following this process, I will provide a brief analysis of the historical trends in Canadian broadcast policy. This portion of [the viewpoint] will outline the protectionist past of our national broadcast policy and illustrate the recent technological and economic developments that now behoove its evolution. Finally, this [viewpoint] will conclude with arguments in support of cultural nationalism as the ideal means to achieve Canada's cultural objectives in today's complicated and internationally oriented broadcast landscape.

Defining Culture

In order to give the forthcoming discussion an optimum sense of clarity, I will begin by defining culture and addressing its value. My word processor's dictionary aptly defines culture as, "the beliefs, customs, practices, and social behaviour of a particular nation or group of people" (Microsoft). Based on this definition, I shall define cultural policy as any government action or position that relates to matters of culture. More specifically, I shall define broadcast cultural policy as any government action or position that relates to the radio or television broadcast of any cultural expression. Considered on their own, these terms are easily understood, however, the challenge lies in their coalescence.

We can all agree that cultural endeavors have numerous benefits both to individuals and to society as a whole. Examples of such benefits range from job creation and nation building to spiritual growth and straightforward entertainment. A vibrant culture is a vital component of any successful and progressive society and the importance of establishing and maintaining such a culture cannot be overstated. While we know that we must diligently manage our culture, ours is a society that has prospered by applying [as Mike Gasher has written] "market economics as the legitimate form of governance" over numerous economic structures and social organizations. Thus, there exists a tendency to assume that the free market can effectively govern anything that we set its sights on. Given this tendency and our government's history of bureaucratic bloat, one is compelled to ask, why should the government involve itself in culture?

[Tyler] Cowen [in *In Praise of Commercial Culture*] points out that a healthy capitalist economy "generates the wealth that enables individuals to support themselves through art." Although Cowen limits his observation to art, his statement rings true for all cultural products. There is no doubt that a prosperous economy full of prosperous individuals creates the money and the time for society to consume culture. However, while the free market stimulates cultural consumption, it is less effective at engendering cultural development. As the broadcasting industry demonstrates, when left on its own, market-based cultural production tends to grow formulaic and homogeneous. In a purely free market, cultural producers, like everyone else, will likely strive to create conditions of predictability and stability within their businesses, as these conditions lend themselves to higher standards of living. Subsequently, many cultural workers will be inclined to rely on proven and more widely accepted production techniques and venture to new creative ground only when past modes of production stagnate. Although the free market rewards diversity in the long run, when cultural producers must rely solely on current public demand for their day-to-day existence, the high short-term risk involved in implementing new modes of production creates little incentive for diversity.

Clash Between Culture and Marketplace

Culture develops best when cultural producers are given room to develop and evolve their ideas through a dialectic of discussion, critique and creativity. Yet, with a necessary focus on competition, efficiency, and fiscal responsibility, conditions of an ideal free market often run counter to the requirements of optimum cultural development. Particularly in their early stages, cultural activities require encouragement and stimulus from a source whose only interests are cultural. While far from perfect, with its capacity to create and fund arm's length policies and institutions, the government is well positioned to intervene and act as such a cultural steward. This is not to say however, that government intervention ought to create a bubble of artsy unaccountability. Rather, under this model, government efforts would provide a buffer intended to help cultural endeavors transition and contribute successfully to the open market.

Aside from the previously mentioned incompatibilities between culture and the free market that transcend political borders, Canada has a second and unique factor that necessitates government involvement in the cultural sphere. As [John] Meisel and [Jean] van Loon observe [in "Cultivating the Bush Garden: Cultural Policy in Canada"], "being a new and postcolonial community, Canada [lacks] a strong tradition of royal, aristocratic, and even private patronage of the arts." In other words, while European nations rely on much older and more culturally ingrained models of cultural support, Canadians have no such means or tradition. Moreover, while Canada has many generous cultural patrons, the Canadian cultural landscape has never experienced American-style cultural philanthropy. Subsequently, in Canada, the onus for cultural support falls to the government, in some regards, by default.

Establishing Objectives

Once one accepts the need for government involvement in the nation's cultural affairs, there arises a corollary to the debate, which concerns the specific objectives of government intervention into the cultural realm. It is not sufficient to say that, since culture benefits everyone and since culture cannot be sustained without help, the government ought to jump in and offer carte blanche to the cultural sphere. Due to the size, scope, and costs involved with any government initiative, a clear statement of purpose, which includes measurable objectives, must be established early on in the policy-making process. While for better or worse, the broadcast policies of [Sir John] Aird [chairman of the Royal Commission on Radio Broadcasting] and [Vincent] Massey [chairman of the Royal Commission on National Development in the Arts, Letters and Sciences] had nation building as their stated purpose, such assertions of intent have bedeviled the more recent efforts of Canadian cultural policy makers. For instance, in an effort to help clarify the intent of Canadian cultural policy, in 1982, the Canada Council [for the Arts] asked the Applebaum-Hébert Committee whether cultural policy should "pursue industrial or cultural objectives." Unfortunately, four years later, the Caplan-Sauvageau report observed that the answer to this question remained "shrouded in ambiguity and confusion." [Rowland] Lorimer and [Nancy] Duxbury would like to concur with the Caplan-Sauvageau report as they argue [in a 1994 article in the *Canadian Journal of Communication*], "a fully articulated philosophy of cultural development has never been developed in Canada."

In their efforts to justify and define objectives for government intervention, there has been a tendency amongst cultural policy makers to pigeonhole cultural benefits according to either a "culturalist discourse" or an "economic discourse." The culturalists hold that "cultural production (is) first and foremost a cultural activity," whose benefits relate primarily to the creation of a more enlightened society, while the economic perspective "defines cultural production as (a) commercial enterprise," with economic benefits. This practice has led to the creation of poorly balanced policy that is susceptible to criticism from whichever side of the culturalist versus economist argument that it fails to address. If policy emanates from a cultural discourse, it "contradicts in fundamental ways the thinking which today guides and constrains government decision making," while if policy is derived from an economic discourse, it raises doubt about the government's true motivations.

Further confounding matters, many in the public feel largely excluded and detached from the creation of appropriate cultural policy. With regards to broadcast cultural policy, [Frank] Peers [in Gordon Fearn's "The Role of Communications Policy in Modern Culture," in *Reflections on Cultural Policy: Past, Present, and Future*] notes that Canadians, "never made a clear choice between broadcasting as 'public service' and broadcasting as a commercial medium and predominantly the purveyor of light entertainment." With this tradition of ambiguity and confusion, it is of little wonder that so many recommendations on cultural policy fall by the wayside. In order to cease this trend, it is my contention that to be effective, modern cultural policy must be subjected to a set of criteria that acknowledge both cultural and economic requirements.

Types of Government Intervention

An act of government intervention into the cultural sphere can take two forms, protectionist or nationalist. These are essentially defensive or offensive courses of action. On one hand, protectionism tends to spawn reactive policies, which are focused on creating an artificial cultural environment within a nation. While on the other hand, nationalist broadcast policies proactively stimulate the creation, and facilitate the consumption of a nation's cultural products.

Ignoring the notion that the "cultural expression is vastly enriched by the free flow of ideas across borders," protectionism's arbitrary restrictions freeze cultural output "like flies in amber." Canada's assorted content requirements, which force private broadcasters to include a certain amount of Canadian content within their daily programming schedules, are our nation's best-known protectionist measures. Although such content restrictions were first introduced in the Broadcasting Act of 1958, Canada has a long history of broadcast protectionism. For instance, both the Aird Commission of 1929 and the Massey-Lévesque Commission of 1951 supported the move to end private national broadcasting. Rather than fostering a balanced market of commercial and public broadcast fare, these commissions suggested that the CBC [Canadian Broadcasting Corporation], as well as its precursor the Canadian Radio Broadcasting Corporation, ought to control everything on the nation's airwaves.

Implementing Positive Policies

While the ivory tower of protectionism is a derivative of fear, well-articulated nationalist policies are the product of confidence and pride. The work of the Applebaum-Hébert Committee serves as an excellent example of nationalist policy making in action. [Mike] Gasher remarks the committee "refused a protectionist stance, preferring to recommend proactive strategies." The committee acknowledged the importance of cultural production by suggesting, that "when creative activity is diminished because many artists are unable to earn a decent living, something is lost to all of us, and our entire culture fails to fulfill its promise." However, rather than positioning itself as the great defender of Canadian morality, Applebaum et al. placed the government in a role of cultural facilitator by arguing that "the essential task of government in

How Does the MAPL System Work?

To qualify as Canadian content, a musical selection must generally fulfill at least two of the following conditions:

- *M* (music): the music is composed entirely by a Canadian

- *A* (artist): the music is, or the lyrics are, performed principally by a Canadian

- *P* (performance): the musical selection consists of a live performance that is

  recorded wholly in Canada, or
  performed wholly in Canada and broadcast live in Canada

- *L* (lyrics): the lyrics are written entirely by a Canadian

Canadian Radio-television
and Telecommunications Commission, 2010.
www.crtc.gc.ca.

cultural matters is to remove obstacles [and] enlarge opportunities." Rather than fighting Americanized mass culture, which Canada is as much a part of as any other Western nation, the committee suggested ways for Canadians to "capitalize upon the American-dominated industrial infrastructure." Examples of successful polices modeled in this spirit include the government sponsored tax benefits and cash subsidies that have supported various Canadian television productions, music videos, and awards shows.

With their shared language, similar cultures, tightly integrated economies and close geographic proximity, Canada and the U.S. have a unique and complicated relationship. By evolving next to the world's largest producer of broadcast culture, Canada's broadcasting policy has long been challenged in ways many other nations are just beginning to understand. Whereas today's satellite and Internet technologies distribute various national broadcasts globally, Canadian audiences have been happily consuming terrestrially based American broadcasts since the days of the first consumer radios. And, since that time, someone in the Canadian government has been working to protect Canadians from American broadcasts.

In the discussion that is to follow, it is not my intent to downplay the efforts of those who have endeavored to foster a diverse and creative cultural spirit in Canada. Nor do I disagree with [Northrop] Frye's assertion that, within global consciousness, it is "of immense importance that there should be other views [than that of the United States] of the human occupation of this continent." However, it is my position that Canadian cultural policy has been co-opted by an overly moral political agenda concerned first, with nation building and later, with strengthening and maintaining a national identity.

When Aird called the "power and penetration of American (radio) stations" the "greatest threat of all" to Canadian culture, he helped make America the great foil to Canada's cultural aspirations that it is today. As any leader knows, one of the best ways to unite disparate groups is to focus them on something that they are all not. If a group can agree that, they are all definitely not some other group, than they have something in common. At the time of the Aird Commission, Canada was a relatively young and developing nation challenged by the need to unite a diverse population that was spread, sometimes thinly, across a large geographic area. In short, commonality was in short supply. By introducing into the policy discourse "two recurrent topics: commercialization and Americanization" or that which would be labeled "other" to the goals of Canadian broadcasting and morality, Aird brought to the national debate something that Canadians, or at least the Canadian elite, could rally around.

From the Aird Commission on, Canadian broadcast policy has been predicated on the need to create and maintain national unity. As Aird famously likened a national broadcasting system to a national railway, the Massey report observed culture's capacity to "help to develop Canadian spirit without raising questions of race, religion or political convictions." Over 40 years later, politicians were singing the same refrain, with the Liberals declaring "national unity and cultural sovereignty as the goal for federal cultural institutions and policy." [Joyce] Zemans summarizes the long-standing character of Canadian broadcasting by suggesting that "the continual Canadian search for identity", "the question of nationhood and . . . the constant presence of the U.S." have been key factors "in shaping Canadian cultural policy."

While the intent of Canadian cultural policy has often been noble, it is a prime illustration of how valid nationalist goals can give way to counterproductive protectionist policies. There are indeed many successful examples of successful nationalism within Canadian cultural policy. The CBC for instance, with its capacity to provide a forum for the display and discussion of Canadian culture, represents nationalist policy at its best. However, with the ongoing Canadian content debate and various government debacles such as the CRTC's [Canadian Radio-television and Telecommunications Commission's] handling of satellite television in the mid-1990s, Canada's dark cloud of broadcasting protectionism lingers. [Paul] Rutherford concludes that the "predominant traits of Canada's cultural industries" are "a hankering for protectionism and a fear of free trade."

The ineffectiveness of protectionism coupled with the need for some sort of government cultural intervention is justification enough for nationalist cultural policy. However, there are also deep-seated technological and economic reasons that make the protectionist leanings of the Aird, Hassey-Lévesque and Fowler reports "no longer adequate to rationalize state governance of the cultural sphere."

Examples of factors that are now, and will in the future, contribute to the unsustainability of protectionist cultural polices could themselves fill several more essays, however, I will briefly summarize two of the most poignant factors. First, from a technological view, the decentralization and the disintermediation that characterizes today's satellite and Web-enabled broadcasting landscape have made the notion of one body deciding a nation's broadcast diet impossible. It seems that the CRTC recognized this sometime ago in stating that, "containing the spread of U.S. broadcast services in Canada [was] workable in 1975 [however, it] is no longer applicable in the changed environment of 1985." Secondly, economically, trade liberalization has placed cultural protectionism at odds with accepted practices of international relations. While Canada must be "vigilant about its right to intervene in the cultural sector," if we want to reap the benefits of global diversity, we must be prepared to open our cultural markets to outsiders. Admittedly, culture will always be a contentious issue within international relations and it is certainly not acceptable to judge trade in culture as one would trade in other goods. However, as trade and culture grow progressively more intertwined and as more cultural productions result from international collaborations, protectionism will become impossible to sustain. The sooner nations acknowledge the need to negotiate cultural interactions, the better prepared their cultures will be to adapt to and develop from broadened global relations.

Protectionism in Canadian cultural policy has failed. Canadian content has become "not representative of Canadian tastes but of a particular class interest." The "vast majority of television viewers [have] neither sought, nor liked, nor consumed" Canadian content, while on the radio, Canadian content is regularly blamed for contributing to the mediocrity of Canada's popular music scene. However, past the fact most Canadians seem to prefer "imported American entertainment," protectionism's failure demonstrates an important truth about the relationship between culture and politics. [Richard] Collins observes that, although Canadian broadcast policies have failed, Canada, as a political unit has been able to persist. Thus, Collins concludes, "polity and culture need not be congruent." In other words, while government efforts to artificially grow culture through primarily protectionist measures have failed, Canada and Canadian identity have grown and prospered. This demonstrates that not only can political ends be achieved independently of cultural conditions, the practice of binding cultural policy with political strategy is ineffective.

As Collins' observation suggests, we are now presented with an opportunity to divest cultural policy of its political agenda and trust in culture's ability to contribute autonomously to society. I have demonstrated the importance of culture and the need for government involvement in its development and I have shown protectionism to be both undesirable and ineffective. Cultural nationalism has already met with great success in Canada. Based on this past performance and their ability to support development while respecting the need for diversity and competition, nationalist policies are a sustainable and desirable means to achieve the continued growth of Canada's unique, diverse, and vibrant culture.

> "If a woman's choice is to wear a niqab, BARRING her from wearing one by removing access to work, child care, health care and education is the absolute opposite of gender equality."

Quebec Should Not Ban the Niqab

Thea Lim

Thea Lim is the deputy editor of Racialious, *a collaborative weblog discussing media coverage of the multiracial community. In the following viewpoint, she contends that Quebec's proposed ban on the niqab will only succeed in refusing essential services to a small minority of women who have chosen to wear it. Lim argues that protecting a woman's right to wear a niqab is true gender equality.*

As you read, consider the following questions:

1. Under Bill 94, what essential services will be denied to women wearing the niqab?

2. What does Lim feel the debate about the niqab ban is really about?

Thea Lim, "Quebec Niqab Ban: No/Non to Bill 94!" Racialious.com, April 7, 2010. Reprinted with permission.

3. What do polls show about the Canadian public's position on the bill?

Last week [April 2010] Jean Charest, premier of the province of Quebec in Canada, proposed legislation that would ban Muslim women from wearing the niqab/face veil.

How does Quebec intend to ban the niqab? By refusing essential services to women wearing one. From the *Toronto Star*:

> [Bill 94] effectively bars Muslim women from receiving or delivering public services while wearing a niqab. According to the draft law, they would not be able to consult a doctor in a hospital, for example, or even attend classes in a university. "Two words: Uncovered face," Charest told reporters during a press conference in Quebec City. "The principle is clear." However, Charest reaffirmed the right to wear other religious symbols, such as crosses, skullcaps or head scarves, which was met by some as evidence of hypocrisy and discrimination. . . .
>
> Charest explained that the legislation, Bill 94, demands a face in plain view, for reasons of identification, security and communication. He further clarified that even public service employees who do not interact with the public—the majority of the provincial bureaucracy—would also not be permitted to wear the niqab. . . .
>
> The legislation doesn't stop at driver's licence or health card offices. It encompasses nearly every public and para-public institution as well, including universities, school boards, hospitals, community health and daycare centres.

There are many things about this bill that are horrendous. For example, that whole universal health care thing—of which many Canadians are so proud—will become pretty UNuniversal; since if you're wearing a niqab you can't see a doctor. Bill 94 returns us to suffragette era politics, where some women (i.e., white ones) got the vote while others didn't; since if you're wearing a niqab you can't vote.

To me one of the most appalling things about Bill 94 is that it is actually being sold as a gender equity thing. More from the *Star*:

> Critics of the niqab say they subjugate women and their right to equality. After a woman was removed this month from a French language class for refusing to remove her niqab, Christine St-Pierre, Quebec's minister responsible for the status of women, called niqabs "ambulatory prisons." On Wednesday, St-Pierre said Quebec was a "world leader" when it comes to gender equality, and with Bill 94, "we prove it once again."

How many times does it have to be said that gender equity is about giving women the right to make their own choices? If a woman's choice is to wear a niqab, BARRING her from wearing one by removing access to work, child care, health care and education is the absolute opposite of gender equality.

I cannot say enough how disgusting and dishonest this is. If this bill was motivated by a real concern for women made to wear the niqab against their will, wouldn't it make more sense to partner with organisations for Muslim women and/or organisations for women fleeing abuse and violence?

Instead, this legislation is being championed primarily by white men and women who are not Muslim.

Since I am getting too apoplectic to be articulate, let's see what other people are saying about Bill 94.

The Non/No Bill 94 Coalition writes in [its] statement:

> Bill 94, if approved, will perpetuate gender inequality by legislating control over women's bodies and sanctioning discrimination against Muslim women who wear the niqab. Instead of singling out a minuscule percentage of the population, government resources would be better spent implementing poverty reduction and education programs to address real gender inequality in meaningful ways. Barring any woman from social services, employment, health, and

education, as well as creating a climate of shame and fear around her is not an effective means to her empowerment. . . . "Rescuing" women is paternalistic and insulting. Further marginalizing Muslim women who wear niqab and denying them access to social services, economic opportunities and civic participation is unacceptable.

Forcing a woman to reveal part of her body is no different from forcing her to be covered.

Jessica writing for *Bitch* points out the silliness of the whole "identity theft" defense, and also asks why there aren't more feminists getting het up about this:

"Let's be honest. The majority of identity theft is done by people WITHOUT head coverings. To date there hasn't been any records of impersonation by someone wearing a niqab."

Now the intersection—what are feminists saying about this issue?

To me this is an obvious feminist issue through and through, and it goes way beyond a human rights injustice. I'm checking myself as an ally to Muslim women, and supporting their right to bodily autonomy and self-determination.

However I'll tell you this much—the amount of mainstream feminist response I've read regarding the lack of inclusion of contraception and abortion in maternal child health from Canada's Conservative government in the G8 [Group of Eight, an intergovernmental organization consisting of the world's leading industrialized nations] summit far exceeds the coverage I've seen regarding the niqab ban. In fact, I've barely seen any feminist press at all on the niqab ban. And I'm not surprised—reproductive rights get lots of feminist attention, even if not mainstream media coverage. Intersecting race and culture? Not so much.

Krista at Muslimah Media Watch quotes a few statistics that bring to light the completely unnecessary nature of Bill 94:

The only thing I want to do here is highlight part of this article, which puts into context just how overblown the whole issue is:

One Muslim group argued Wednesday that Quebec's political oxygen was being unnecessarily sucked up by debate over a microscopic number of cases.

The Muslim Council of Montreal says there may be only around 25 Muslims in Quebec who actually wear face coverings.

Of the more than 118,000 visitors to the health board's Montreal office in 2008–09 only 10 people—or less than 0.00009 per cent of cases—involved niqab wearers who asked for special dispensation. There were zero such cases among the 28,000 visitors to the Quebec City service centre over the same time period.

So, everyone who's freaking out about how Quebecois culture as we know it is going to crumble if people are allowed to wear niqab can probably breathe easy.

Quebec is using precious voter time and money (and let me tell you, as a Canadian that money really is precious—Canada's social resources are notoriously stretched) to cause a national (perhaps international) scandal over 25 women.

So again, let's be honest. This is not about the 25 women in Quebec who wear niqabs. Like the minaret ban is Switzerland or the burqa ban in France, (and these legislations similarly kick up a huge amount of fuss over a tiny portion of the population), this is about Islamophobia, xenophobia [fear of foreigners] and racism, of which Quebec (and Canada) has a rich and storied history. . . .

The worst part yet? Polls suggest a majority of Canadians support this bill.

Please visit, forward and join the Non/No Bill 94 Coalition. [Its] website is here, and this is [its] full statement:

Discriminating Against Women

Shelina Merani, a spokesperson for Muslim Presence, a network promoting common values based on Islam, charged that the bill [Bill 94, which would ban face coverings such as the niqab] is discriminatory and reflects growing anti-Muslim sentiment in Quebec.

"As a woman, you will have to choose between your education and our faith," Merani said in an interview from Ottawa.

"If we want to emancipate women, I think this will do the opposite of what we claim to want to do—it will contribute to ghettoization," she said.

Cris Bouroncle,
"Red Flag on Quebec Niqab Ban,"
Montreal Gazette, *March 26, 2010.*

Quebec Premier Jean Charest has proposed legislation which, if approved by the National Assembly of Quebec, would deny essential government services, public employment, educational opportunities, and health care to people who wear facial coverings. Bill 94 specifically targets Muslim women who wear the niqab (face veil). The bill is an exaggerated response to a manufactured crisis that will allow the government to deny women services to which they are entitled. A truly democratic society is one in which all individuals have the freedom of religious expression and a right to access public services.

Although touted as a step toward gender equality, Bill 94, if approved, will perpetuate gender inequality by legislating control over women's bodies and sanctioning discrimination against Muslim women who wear the niqab. Instead of singling out a minuscule percentage of the population, government resources would be better spent implementing poverty reduction and education programs to address real gender inequality in meaningful ways. Barring any woman from social services, employment, health, and education as well as creating a climate of shame and fear around her is not an effective means to her empowerment. If Premier Charest's government is truly committed to gender equality it should foster a safe and inclusive society which promotes and protects all women's personal autonomy. Standing up for women's rights is admirable. "Rescuing" women is paternalistic and insulting. Further marginalizing Muslim women who wear niqab and denying them access to social services, economic opportunities and civic participation is unacceptable.

Forcing a woman to reveal part of her body is no different from forcing her to be covered. Both the Conservative and Liberal parties have expressed support for Bill 94, which raises the very real possibility that similar legislation will be proposed across Canada. We demand that Bill 94 be withdrawn immediately, as it has no place in a democratic state that values autonomy, liberty and justice.

We invite all individuals and groups of conscience inside and outside of Quebec to publicly or privately endorse this statement by emailing their name(s), location (city, state/province, and country), and contact information to non-bill94 [at] gmail [dot] com

The Non/No Bill 94 Coalition is made up of concerned individuals, organizations and grassroots movements that are demanding that the proposed Quebec legislation, Bill 94, be withdrawn immediately.

Periodical and Internet Sources Bibliography

The following articles have been selected to supplement the diverse views presented in this chapter.

Daphne Bramham — "Let's Not Mistake Oppression for Fashion Choices," *Vancouver Sun*, August 11, 2010.

Chuck Colson — "What's the Matter with Canada?" Townhall.com, July 21, 2008. http://townhall.com.

Ann Coulter — "Oh, Canada!" AnnCoulter.com, March 24, 2010. www.anncoulter.com.

Tarek Fatah — "Ban the Niqab," The Mark, April 15, 2010. www.themarknews.com.

Kevin Michael Grace — "What Canada's Free Speech Victory Says About America's Matthew Shepard 'Hate Crimes' Bill," VDARE.com, September 3, 2009. www.vdare.com.

Norma Greenaway — "Nothing Is Simple About Controversy Inspired by a Simple Veil Known as Niqab," *Vancouver Sun*, August 13, 2010.

Ezra Levant — "Time to Face Facts on Burkas," *Ottawa Sun*, August 1, 2010.

Rich Lowry — "Gagged in Canada: Speech Police Run Amok," Real Clear Politics, June 10, 2008. www.realclearpolitics.com.

Megan O'Toole — "'Concern' over Veiled Passengers," *National Post*, August 3, 2010.

Jordan Michael Smith — "Canada's Clampdown on Free Speech," *Boston Globe*, March 27, 2010.

Mark Warren — "In Defense of Ann Coulter," *Esquire*, March 24, 2010.

CHAPTER 4

What Issues Are Impacting Canada– US Relations?

Chapter Preface

On July 27, 2002, the US military engaged in a ferocious firefight with militant forces in the village of Ayub Kheyl, Afghanistan, a region in the eastern part of the country known to be sympathetic to the Taliban. After four hours of fighting, a young man named Omar Khadr was captured by US forces; it was quickly discovered that Khadr was a Canadian citizen and only fifteen years old at the time of his capture—a child soldier. Khadr was transferred to the Guantánamo Bay Naval Base in October 2002. He was designated as an "enemy combatant" and an al Qaeda fighter at a hearing in 2004. He was accused of war crimes and killing a US soldier by throwing a hand grenade during combat, planting mines to target US convoys, and gathering surveillance at an Afghan airport. The only Western citizen remaining in Guantánamo, he is also the youngest prisoner there.

Over the past few years, Khadr has become a cause célèbre in Canada. Because the Canadian government has refused to seek extradition or repatriation, some organizations and critics began to accuse it of failing to protect a Canadian citizen, especially when he had reportedly been tortured in American custody. Amnesty International, UNICEF (United Nations Children's Fund), the Canadian Bar Association, and other influential political and legal organizations repeatedly urged the Canadian government to act. Even more controversy erupted when it was revealed that the Canadian government had spent more than $1.3 million to keep Khadr in Guantánamo.

Forces in Canada, however, were ready to investigate the matter. In 2009 a review concluded that the Canadian Cabinet had failed Khadr by ignoring his juvenile status and his allegations of abuse and torture at the hands of the US military at Guantánamo. That same year, the Canadian courts weighed in. The Federal Court of Canada determined that the Canadian Charter of Rights and Freedoms obligated the government to demand Khadr's return. A court of appeals concurred with that decision. When the case went to the Supreme Court of Canada, it ruled that although Khadr's constitutional rights had been violated, the government was not obligated to demand his return to Canada.

That decision did nothing in Canada to quell the outrage surrounding the Khadr case. Critics of the government's inaction continued to fight for Canada to intervene in the case. They point to the fact that most of the evidence against him is based on a series of confessions Khadr made under torture and at the age of fifteen. His defense lawyers argue that Khadr was only a child left with al Qaeda by his radical father and ordered to be their translator. Supporters of the government's policy argued that Khadr had received a fair trial and that Canada must respect the legal process of the United States. Political commentators also point out that Canada does not want to interfere because in 1995 the Canadian government had interfered in the case of Ahmed Said Khadr, Omar's father, which resulted in his release from Pakistani custody and his eventual support of Osama bin Laden and al Qaeda.

Public opinion on the Khadr matter was divided. According to Angus Reid Public Opinion, 36 percent believed that Khadr should be repatriated to Canada as of July 2010. In addition, "more than half of Canadians (52%) say they do not feel sympathy for Omar Khadr's plight, while one-third (34%) do sympathize with Khadr's situation."

The controversial case of Omar Khadr is one of several topics covered in the following chapter, which focuses on the relationship between Canada and the United States. Other viewpoints include discussion on the impact of American security policies on Canada, water policy, and the state of Canada's special relationship with its southern neighbor.

> *"Canada views good relations with the U.S. as crucial to a wide range of interests, and often looks to the U.S. as a common cause partner promoting democracy, transparency, and good governance around the world."*

Canada and the United States Still Have a "Special Relationship"

US Department of State

The US Department of State is responsible for coordinating the international relations of the United States. In the following viewpoint, the close relationship between Canada and the United States is detailed, including instances in which Canadian policies have opposed American ones. Overall, the State Department describes the relationship as "the closest and most extensive in the world."

As you read, consider the following questions:

1. How many people cross the US-Canada border every day?

US Department of State, "Background Note: Canada," February 18, 2010. Reprinted with permission.

177

2. How many Canadian military forces are deployed in Afghanistan?

3. What is the Clean Energy Dialogue?

The relationship between the United States and Canada is the closest and most extensive in the world. It is reflected in the staggering volume of bilateral trade—the equivalent of $1.6 billion a day in goods—as well as in people-to-people contact. About 300,000 people cross the shared border every day.

A 2004 law has phased in new rules for travel between Canada and the United States. Since January 2007, U.S. citizens traveling by air to and from Canada have needed a valid passport to enter or re-enter the United States. Beginning January 31, 2008, U.S. and Canadian citizens aged 19 and older traveling into the U.S. from Canada by land or sea (including ferries) have had to present documents denoting citizenship and identity. This change primarily affects American and Canadian citizens who had previously been permitted entry into the U.S. by oral declaration alone, and marks the transition toward standard and consistent documents for all travelers entering the U.S. Acceptable documentation includes a valid passport or government-issued photo identification such as a driver's license and proof of citizenship such as a birth certificate. Children aged 18 and under need only to present a birth certificate.... Travelers who do not present acceptable documents may be delayed as U.S. Customs and Border Protection officers at the port of entry attempt to verify identity and citizenship. Since June 2009, all travelers, including U.S. citizens, have had to present a passport or other secure document that denotes identity and citizenship when entering the U.S. from Canada.

A Close Relationship

In fields ranging from law enforcement to environmental protection to free trade, the two countries work closely on multiple levels from federal to local. In addition to their close bilateral ties, Canada and the U.S. cooperate in multilateral fora. Canada—a charter signatory to the United Nations and the North Atlantic Treaty Organization (NATO), and a member of the G8 and G-20 [Group of Eight and Group of Twenty, fora for the governments of the world's major economies that hold annual summits]—takes an active role in the United Nations, including peacekeeping operations, and participates in the Organization for Security and Co-operation in Europe (OSCE). Canada joined the Organization of American States (OAS) in 1990 and hosted the OAS General Assembly in Windsor in June 2000, and the third Summit of the Americas in Quebec City in April 2001. Canada seeks to expand its ties to Pacific Rim economies through membership in the Asia-Pacific Economic Cooperation forum (APEC), and hosted the Winter Olympic Games in Vancouver-Whistler, British Columbia, in 2010.

Canada views good relations with the U.S. as crucial to a wide range of interests, and often looks to the U.S. as a common cause partner promoting democracy, transparency, and good governance around the world. Nonetheless, it sometimes pursues policies at odds with our own. Canada decided in 2003 not to contribute troops to the U.S.-led military coalition in Iraq (although it later contributed financially to Iraq's reconstruction and provided electoral advice). Other recent examples are: Canada's leadership in the creation of the UN [United Nations]-created International Criminal Court (ICC) for war crimes; its decision in early 2005 not to participate directly in the U.S. missile defense program; and its strong support for the Ottawa Convention [Ottawa Treaty, or the Convention on the Prohibition of the Use, Stockpiling, Production and Transfer of Anti-Personnel Mines and on Their Destruction] to ban anti-personnel mines. The U.S., while the world's leading supporter of demining initiatives, declined to sign the treaty due to unmet concerns regarding the protection of its forces and allies, particularly those serving on the Korean Peninsula, as well as the lack of exemptions for mixed munitions.

Defense Issue

U.S. defense arrangements with Canada are more extensive than with any other country. The Permanent Joint Board on Defense, established in 1940, provides policy-level consultation on bilateral defense matters and the U.S. and Canada share NATO mutual security commitments. In addition, U.S. and Canadian military forces have cooperated since 1958 on continental air defense within the framework of the North American Aerospace Defense Command (NORAD). The military response to the September 11, 2001, terrorist attacks in the United States both tested and strengthened military cooperation between the U.S. and Canada. The new NORAD agreement that entered into force on May 12, 2006, added a maritime domain awareness component and is of "indefinite duration," albeit subject to periodic review. Since 2002, Canada has participated in diplomatic, foreign assistance, and joint military actions in Afghanistan. Approximately 2,500 Canadian Forces personnel are deployed at any given time in southern Afghanistan under a battle group based at Kandahar and as members of the Canadian-led Provincial Reconstruction Team (PRT) at Camp Nathan Smith in Kandahar. The Canadian Parliament has approved the extension of this mission in Kandahar until 2011. Canada has also contributed to stabilization efforts in Haiti, initially with troops and later with civilian police and electoral assistance, and humanitarian and developmental aid.

Environmental Issues

The U.S. and Canada also work closely to resolve transboundary environmental issues, an area of increasing importance in the bilateral relationship. A principal instrument of this cooperation is the International Joint Commission (IJC), established as part of the Boundary Waters Treaty of 1909 to resolve differences and promote international cooperation on boundary waters; Secretary of State Hillary Clinton and Foreign [Affairs] Minister Lawrence Cannon celebrated the treaty's centenary in June 2009. The Great Lakes Water Quality Agreement of 1978 (as amended in 1987) is another historic example of joint cooperation in controlling trans-boundary water pollution; President Barack Obama's administration has committed itself, along with Canada, to update the agreement. The two governments also consult regularly on trans-boundary air pollution. Under the Air Quality Agreement of 1991, both countries have made substantial progress in coordinating and implementing their acid rain control programs and signed an annex on ground level ozone in 2000.

Canada ratified the Kyoto accord [Kyoto Protocol, a treaty whereby countries agree to reduce greenhouse gases] in 2002, despite concern among business groups and others that compliance would place Canada's economy at a lasting competitive disadvantage vis-à-vis the U.S. Prime Minister Stephen Harper's government announced in 2006, however, that Canada would not be able to meet its original Kyoto Protocol commitments. In April 2007, the Canadian Government announced a new regulatory framework for greenhouse gas emissions that was to be implemented beginning in 2010; however, progress on that framework has been somewhat slower than anticipated and the implementation date has slipped to 2012. Moreover, since late 2008 Canada has emphasized that it would prefer to see a harmonized cap-and-trade regime and coordinated greenhouse gas emissions reduction plan for both Canada and the United States. In February 2009 President Obama and Prime Minister Harper announced the bilateral Clean Energy Dialogue (CED), which is charged with expanding clean energy research and development; developing and deploying clean energy technology; and building a more efficient electricity grid based on clean and renewable energy in order to reduce greenhouse gases and combat climate change in both countries. U.S. Energy Secretary Steven Chu and Canadian Minister of Environment Jim Prentice serve as the lead government officials for moving the Clean Energy Dialogue forward.

Canada also participates in the U.S.-led Major Economies Forum on Energy and Climate, which includes the world's 17 largest economies as well as the UN; the Asia-Pacific Partnership on Clean Development and Climate, which joins it with the U.S., Japan, Australia, South Korea, China, and India in a broad effort to accelerate the development and deployment of clean energy technologies in major industrial sectors; and the international Carbon Sequestration Leadership Forum, which researches effective ways to capture and store carbon dioxide.

Border Issues

While bilateral law enforcement cooperation and coordination were excellent prior to the September 11, 2001, terrorist attacks in the United States, they have since become even closer through such mechanisms as the Cross-Border Crime Forum. Canada, like the U.S., has strengthened its laws and realigned resources to fight terrorism. U.S.-Canada security cooperation to create a safe and secure border is exemplary. Canadian and U.S. federal and local law enforcement personnel fight cross-border crime through cooperation on joint Integrated Border Enforcement Teams (IBETs). Companies on both sides of the border have joined governments in highly successful partnerships and made massive investments to secure their own facilities and internal supply chains. Over 70% of Canada-U.S. trade is transported by truck. Some commercial drivers crossing the border have volunteered to undergo background security checks under the bilateral Free and Secure Trade (FAST) program and many companies participate in the Customs-

Trade Partnership Against Terrorism (C-TPAT). These initiatives have helped secure trade while speeding border processing.

Canada is a significant source of marijuana and synthetic drugs (methamphetamines, ecstasy) reaching the U.S., as well as precursor chemicals and over-the-counter drugs used to produce illicit synthetic drugs. Implementation and strengthening of regulations in Canada and increased U.S.-Canadian law enforcement cooperation have had a substantial impact in reducing trafficking in precursor chemicals and synthetic drugs, but cannabis cultivation, because of its profitability and relatively low risk of penalty, remains a thriving industry. Canada increased maximum penalties for methamphetamine offenses in August 2005 and implemented new controls over various precursors in November 2005. Canada is active in international efforts to combat terrorist financing and money laundering.

Canada's Foreign Aid Policies

Canada is a large foreign aid donor and targets its annual assistance of C$4.4 billion toward priority sectors such as good governance; health (including HIV/AIDS [human immunodeficiency virus/acquired immune deficiency syndrome]); basic education; private sector development; and environmental sustainability. Canada is a major aid donor to Iraq, Haiti, and Afghanistan.

Prime Minister Harper, who entered office stating he intended to bring a new, more positive tone to bilateral relations while still defending Canadian interests, held his first meeting with President Obama in Ottawa on February 19, 2009. Harper visited Washington September 15–17, 2009. The two leaders have also met several times at multilateral events, including the North American Leaders' summit in Guadalajara, Mexico, in July 2009, and the G-20 summit in Pittsburgh in September 2009.

| "Canadians have always expected a certain special consideration from the United States."

The Canada–US Relationship Has Changed

Brian Bow

Brian Bow is a professor at Dalhousie University, a Fulbright Visiting Research Chair at the Woodrow Wilson International Center for Scholars, and the author of The Politics of Linkage: Power, Interdependence, and Ideas in Canada-US Relations. *In the following viewpoint, he contends that the "special relationship" between the United States and Canada has irrevocably changed. Bow argues that Canada must take into account the global challenges American presidents are dealing with and focus on how to be a constructive global power.*

As you read, consider the following questions:

1. How does the author characterize the working relationship between Canada and the United States during the Cold War?

2. According to the author, what was the turning point in the US-Canada relationship?

Brian Bow, "We Can't Return to Our Special Relationship with the United States," *Globe and Mail*, April 28, 2010. Reprinted with permission.

3. How does Bow believe that Canadian leaders can cultivate strong personal relationships with American counterparts?

A few weeks ago, we were treated to a bit of classic Canadian political theatre. U.S. Secretary of State Hillary Clinton went out of her way to highlight differences between Canadian and American government positions on the Arctic,
Afghanistan and abortion. The comments themselves were not
particularly novel or provocative, but they gave Canadians another opportunity to clash over whether the two countries
share a "special relationship," and what that means for our
foreign policy priorities.

Canadians have always expected a certain special consideration from the United States. No one was ever naive enough
to think that Washington would put Canadian interests ahead
of American ones, but there was an expectation that Canada
would always get a fair hearing, and that the United States
would exercise restraint in dealings with Canada. Yet we are
growing accustomed to U.S. officials criticizing Canadian decisions, and—more often—undertaking new policies without
taking Canadian interests into consideration. We hope our
government can revive the old special relationship, but we
worry they might get too cozy, and we still reward them for
the occasional show of defiance.

There are good reasons to be nostalgic about the way the
bilateral relationship worked in the early Cold War [political
conflict between the United States and the Soviet Union, from
1947–1991] years. There were frictions, but the two governments consistently thought in terms of common interests and
followed tacit "rules of the game," which usually worked to
Canada's advantage. Both still have an interest in sustaining
the symbolism of the special relationship. But things have
changed, and we can't go back to the way things were.

The Turning Point

The turning point wasn't the free trade agreement, the end of the Cold War or 9/11 [the September 11, 2001, terrorist attacks on the United States]. These events shook up the bilateral relationship, but the pivotal moment was really the early 1970s, when the Vietnam War and Watergate [a political scandal that led to the resignation of U.S. president Richard Nixon] smashed the "imperial presidency" and fragmented control over U.S. foreign policy. America's ability to recognize and adhere to postwar diplomatic culture was irretrievably lost, and the relationship became more confrontational, complicated and unpredictable. Thus, it has become harder for Canadian governments to build up goodwill and convert it into concrete diplomatic concessions. Yet some new opportunities have also been created for negotiators to "play" the more fragmented

American system, and thereby influence foreign and domestic policies. The recent wrangling over the Buy American legislation highlighted both the limits on what the executive branch can deliver for Canada, and the value of plugging into the U.S. system at multiple points.

It is still important for Canadian leaders to cultivate strong personal relationships with American counterparts. To do this, we have to demonstrate that we can help them solve their problems, or at least make a credible argument that our problems are also theirs. Prime Minister Stephen Harper has made an effort to build bridges with Barack Obama's administration. But like his recent predecessors, he has tended to harp on the things that Canada wants, with little to say about the global challenges American presidents are most concerned with. (This is partly Mr. Harper's problem, but it is also partly about the long-term decline of Canadian foreign policy and the perils of minority government.) We need to get past worrying about how the United States will react to our switch from a combat to a non-combat role in Afghanistan, and start thinking about what we will do afterward to show that Canada remains a global player.

Canada Should Pursue a Balanced Approach

We cannot, however, lose sight of this strategy's limitations; it has to be embedded in a more "balanced" approach that takes into account the enduring fragmentation of power in Washington. The White House can only do so much to "manage" the bilateral relationship, even at the best of times, and these are very challenging times for Mr. Obama's administration. While seeking stronger ties at the top, Canada must continue to invest in the kinds of diplomatic coping strategies that it struggled to develop in the 1980s and 1990s: building networks and transnational alliances, lobbying Congress, engaging in public diplomacy, grappling with the U.S. legal system, trying to contain American power through formal institutions. That's a lot to ask of a shaky, shortsighted minority government, but there really is no alternative, and the stakes couldn't be higher.

> *"By keeping Khadr in a second-class sys-
> tem and trying him with third-rate evi-
> dence, the Obama administration has
> pretty much guaranteed that the em-
> barrassment over Omar Khadr is only
> just beginning."*

Canada Should Intervene in the Omar Khadr Case

Dahlia Lithwick

Dahlia Lithwick is a senior editor for Slate. *In the following
viewpoint, she chronicles the legal wrangling involved in the
Omar Khadr case, a Canadian citizen who was captured while
fighting in Afghanistan and is scheduled to be tried by an American military commission. Lithwick notes the inaction of Canadian officials—particularly the Canadian Supreme Court—to
intervene in the Khadr case and deems the entire issue an embarrassment for the American government.*

As you read, consider the following questions:

1. How old was Omar Khadr when he was captured by
   American forces?

2. What is Omar Khadr accused of doing?

Dahlia Lithwick, "Supreme Court Dispatch, Eh," *Slate*, November 13, 2009. Reprinted
with permission.

3. According to Robert Frater, a lawyer in Canada's Justice Department, why has the Canadian government declined to seek repatriation of Omar Khadr?

O mar Khadr saw more legal action today [November 13, 2009] in the span of an hour than he's experienced in the seven-plus years he's been held at Guantánamo Bay [a U.S. military detainment facility located in Cuba, also known as "Gitmo"]. Just as Khadr's plight was the subject of an inquiry before the Canadian Supreme Court, which was looking into whether Khadr needs to be forcibly extricated from his American captors, U.S. Attorney General Eric Holder made his American captors appear even more suspicious by announcing that, unlike some of the other detainees at Guantánamo, Khadr will never get a trial in civilian court. If today's oral arguments aren't enough to convince the Canadian Supreme Court to intercede on Khadr's behalf, maybe Holder's announcement will be.

The Story of Omar Khadr

Khadr, a Canadian, was 15 years old when he was captured in Afghanistan for allegedly throwing the grenade that killed a U.S. soldier. Now 23, he is the youngest prisoner and last Westerner at Gitmo. He was awaiting trial there by military commission—a trial that had been stayed by the [Barack] Obama administration until today—when Holder announced that his military trial is on again. Holder also announced that several other detainees will be tried in federal court, ensuring that Khadr will receive second-tier justice while some of his fellow prisoners get the real stuff. Now the question is whether the Supreme Court—that would be Canada's Supreme Court, eh?—can order Khadr home.

Regardless of venue, the case against Khadr will have to contend with some uncomfortable facts. He was captured as a child soldier but offered none of the protections that warranted. Video surfaced last year [2008] of him weeping as he described being abused under detention. Khadr alleges that he has been shackled in stress positions until he wet himself, then used as a "human mop" to clean his own urine. In May 2008, Canada's Supreme Court ruled that Khadr's detention "constituted a clear violation of fundamental human rights protected by international law." And this morning the same court looked at a lower court ruling that demanded the government seek Khadr's repatriation.

The Role of Military Commissions

Meanwhile, south of the border, Holder announced that while five of the Guantánamo detainees implicated in the 9/11 bombings [the September 11, 2001, terrorist attacks on the United States], including Khalid Sheikh Mohammed, will be tried in a federal court in New York City, Khadr and several others will instead face trial before a military commission. As Morris Davis, the former chief prosecutor for the military commissions, argued earlier this week, the forum for each detainee seems to depend on the government's evidence against him. Since military commissions allow weaker evidence (like hearsay and coerced testimony), they are reserved for the weaker cases. Wrote Davis: "The evidence likely to clear the high bar gets gold medal justice: a traditional trial in our federal courts. The evidence unable to clear the federal court standard is forced to settle for a military commission trial, a specially created forum that has faltered repeatedly for more than seven years."

This morning's argument . . . before Canada's Supreme Court is striking. Not just because (unlike arguments before the U.S. Supreme Court) you could see all of its fabulousness on television. And not just because the justices include all sorts of quirky outliers, including women, people with French accents, and men with fantastic hair. (Canada is the kind of place in which Simon Potter, from *Avocats Sans Frontières*, intervening in the case today for Khadr, speaks English with a Scottish accent yet argues his case to the justices in French.) It's mainly striking because Canada, for better or worse, is in a legal conversation with the rest of the world in a way the United States is not.

Throughout oral argument, which lasts all morning, foreign treaties and instruments are cited by both sides. The holdings of foreign courts are referenced, as are special rapporteurs from the United Nations [UN]. The justices struggle to find a link between their international treaty obligations and Canadian domestic law. Everyone concedes that what the rest of the world thinks doesn't decide this case one way or another. But neither do the justices or the lawyers pretend that the rest of the world is a barren legal wasteland.

Harper Fails to Act

Khadr's lawyers won an order from a federal court, reaffirmed by an appeals court, that his rights under the Canadian Charter of Rights and Freedoms were breached when Canadian officials, knowing he'd been tortured, nevertheless interviewed him at Guantánamo. The appeals court ordered that he be repatriated to Canada. Yet Prime Minister Stephen Harper of Canada has not requested repatriation, and the Canadian government warns in this case that no court in the world has ever required that a government intervene to help its citizens detained on foreign soil.

A lawyer from Canada's Justice Department, Robert Frater, tells the court this morning that Khadr's charter rights have not been breached and that "the courts have no more authority to order the government to request repatriation than to order the government to recall an ambassador or amass battleships." Frater says the Canadian government has declined to seek repatriation because Harper "wanted to allow the process in the United States to play out." He says the Canadian government has a "history of asking that Khadr's rights be respected by the United States," but that Khadr has no right to ask the Canadian government to bring him home.

No Obligation to Intervene

Justice Rosalie Silberman Abella—a cross between [Canadian singer] Céline Dion and [U.S. Supreme Court Justice] Ruth Bader Ginsburg—asks why Canada can't be *forced* to repatriate Khadr in the face of "the ongoing intransigence of the American government." Frater says that even under international treaties prohibiting torture, a state has only a discretionary choice to intervene—no affirmative obligation or duty. Justice William Ian Corneil Binnie says the court can step in if there has been a constitutional breach. Frater replies, sassily: "Identify the charter breach and give a remedy if you can find one. But there isn't one!"

Justice Morris J. Fish notes that Frater's time line of the Canadian government's interventions in Khadr's plight ends three and a half years ago. He asks to be updated. Frater says he wasn't trying to hide anything. Says Fish: "I didn't think you were trying to hide anything. I was just asking if you had anything to hide." Frater replies, "I celebrate what's in the record." He says the Canadian government's involvement in questioning a sleep-deprived Khadr is not complicity in torture. And even if the court finds that the Canadian officials' questioning of Khadr violated the charter, the remedy isn't to order Khadr back to Canada. It's not to use the fruits of the interrogation. Since Khadr refused to answer any questions, this isn't a problem. Case closed!

But Abella asks what affirmative duties Canada owes Khadr under another pesky international treaty: the UN Convention on the Rights of the Child. Replies Frater: "If we detained him we'd have full obligations. But we did not." The international treaties are not "self-executing," and for the court to enforce them is to cut the Canadian Parliament out of the picture.

The Case of Omar Khadr

Canadian citizen Omar Khadr was detained by U.S. forces in Afghanistan in July 2002 and transferred to Guantánamo [Bay] Naval Base in October 2002. He was 15 years old when he was taken to Guantánamo and has spent more than a quarter of his life there, now in his eighth year of confinement. Khadr alleges he was repeatedly subjected to torture and cruel treatment during multiple interrogation sessions in U.S. military custody at Bagram Airfield in Afghanistan and at Guantánamo Bay.

Khadr is accused of killing a U.S. soldier with a hand grenade during combat with U.S. forces, planting mines to target U.S. convoys, and gathering surveillance at an airport in Afghanistan. He is the sole detainee at Guantánamo Bay to be charged for acts committed as a juvenile.

Human Rights First,
"The Case of Omar Ahmed Khadr, Canada," 2010.
www.humanrightsfirst.org.

What Are Canada's Obligations?

Binnie asks whether it matters that the United States itself has deemed the conditions of Khadr's detention illegal. Frater replies that the U.S. process has "been fixed." Binnie replies that this is not at all clear. Frater reassures him that someday, Khadr can bring all these complaints up at his U.S. trial.

Nathan Whitling represents Khadr, and his problem is that while the court clearly feels for his client, it can't seem to find a way to bring him home. As he begins to speak, he notes that he has just received an unconfirmed report that his client will be tried by military commission, not in a civilian court. He says, sadly, that it appears Khadr will stay at Gitmo for a long time.

Justice Louise Charron asks whether the charter breach stems from Canada's participation in interrogating Khadr or in an affirmative duty to protect him. Whitling says both. He talks about international law and principles for some time before Charron stops him to ask where his "bridge" is between international and domestic law. Whitling says he is talking here about *jus cogens*—he spells it out slowly, like a good Canadian—which means "norms of international law" and "principles of foundational justice." At this point, I can't help but think that, if this were the U.S. Supreme Court, Justice Antonin Scalia would have run him through with a pointy sword by now. In fact, nobody seems to yell at the lawyers at all this morning—even when Whitling concedes that there aren't a lot of cases to support his point.

Forcing Canada to Act

Whitling rests much of his argument on the fact that Canadian officials knew Khadr was sleep-deprived when they questioned him. But he concedes that Canada didn't seek this state of affairs or cause it to happen. Chief Justice Beverley McLachlin notes that one usually expects a remedy to "fix something up" and that while Khadr "has suffered greatly with great consequences," it's not clear that we can "fix that suffering by bringing him back home." Whitling says repatriating him would offer restitution. McLachlin replies that he should maybe find some cases that say that.

Justice Binnie asks if it would be OK if the court just issued a declaration in the case without ordering the executive to repatriate him. Whitling says, sassily, that "a declaration is of no value whatsoever to Mr. Khadr." Then a whole host of interveners, including Amnesty International, Human Rights Watch, and the Canadian Coalition for the Rights of Children, get time to argue on Khadr's behalf. The court grapples politely together for some principled reason to take the extraordinary step of ordering the Canadian government to take dramatic action in the realm of diplomacy and foreign policy.

A few still appear to hold out hope that Khadr will somehow get a fair trial from their kooky southern neighbors and put an end to this whole embarrassing affair. But Holder's announcement makes that seem ever more unlikely. In fact, by keeping Khadr in a second-class system and trying him with third-rate evidence, the Obama administration has pretty much guaranteed that the embarrassment over Omar Khadr is only just beginning.

> "Arrested in July 2002 following a fire-fight with U.S. forces in Afghanistan, [Omar] Khadr faces five war crimes charges, including murder in the death of a U.S. serviceman."

Canada Is Not Going to Interfere in the Omar Khadr Case

Sheldon Alberts and Steven Edwards

Sheldon Alberts and Steven Edwards are reporters for the Canwest News Service. In the following viewpoint, they report that Canadian officials have provided assurances that they will not interfere in the prosecution of the Omar Khadr case. Alberts and Edwards also describe recent controversies behind the scenes with the case.

As you read, consider the following questions:

1. What Canadian official provided assurances to the Obama administration that Canada would not interfere in the Khadr case?

2. What Canadian Liberal leader pressed Barack Obama to return Khadr to Canada?

Sheldon Alberts and Steven Edwards, "Canada Vows Not to 'Interfere' in Khadr Case," *Edmonton Journal*, February 24, 2009. Reprinted with permission.

3. What does Khadr's lawyer, Lt.-Cmdr. Kuebler, believe should happen to his client?

Foreign Affairs Minister Lawrence Cannon on Tuesday [February 2009] provided assurances to the [Barack] Obama administration Canada will not "interfere" in its review of terrorism charges against Canadian Omar Khadr, the last Westerner remaining at Guantánamo [Bay, a U.S. military detainment facility located in Cuba].

Meanwhile, a row has erupted between Mr. Khadr's military lawyer and the officer's boss—resulting in the lawyer being barred from seeing the Canadian-born terror suspect as an inquiry unfolds.

Mr. Cannon raised Mr. Khadr's case during a meeting in Washington with Secretary of State Hillary Clinton, seeking information about the U.S. decision to conduct a 120-day review of all Guantánamo detainees facing terrorism charges. President Barack Obama ordered an effective suspension of the military commission proceedings against Mr. Khadr until completion of the review.

The Case of Omar Khadr

Mr. Khadr, 22, is accused of throwing a grenade that killed a U.S. army sergeant during a firefight near Khost, Afghanistan, in 2002. At the time of his capture, he was 15 years old and his lawyers argue he cannot face a war crimes trial because he was a child soldier under international law.

"This individual is allegedly a murderer. He is an individual who is allegedly as well accused of terrorism," Mr. Cannon said.

"We have indicated today that the government of Canada fully respects the process that the American government is putting forward." Mr. Cannon added that he told Ms. Clinton "he will not interfere in this process as long as you people have Mr. Khadr under your surveillance."

Mr. Cannon's inquiry on Mr. Khadr's case comes less than a week after Liberal leader Michael Ignatieff pressed Obama—in a brief meeting during the president's visit to Ottawa—for Mr. Khadr to be returned to Canada to face justice.

Controversy Erupts

One of Mr. Obama's first decisions was to announce the closure of the Guantánamo Bay military prison and a review on how to dispense with the remaining detainees—either by repatriating some to their home countries, releasing them or prosecuting them.

Mr. Khadr's lawyer, Navy Lt.-Cmdr. Bill Kuebler, remained in Washington, D.C., Tuesday after being refused a place on the military flight to the U.S. naval base in Cuba's Guantánamo Bay, where Mr. Khadr is in one of the detention camps.

Lt.-Cmdr. Kuebler, who has represented Mr. Khadr since early 2007, charges that the denial to board came after he inquired about a possible "conflict of interest" involving his boss, Air Force Col. Peter Masciola.

"The action effectively denies Omar the right to counsel and constitutes a serious violation of attorney ethics rules," Mr. Kuebler said in a news release.

Khadr's Future Uncertain

In an interview, Lt.-Cmdr. Kuebler said a conflict exists if—as he says he suspects has happened—Col. Masciola has suggested Mr. Khadr now be prosecuted in the U.S. federal system. Lt.-Cmdr. Kuebler has long argued the Toronto-born Khadr, 22, should be repatriated to Canada.

Col. Masciola, who oversees all the Pentagon-appointed defence lawyers for the Guantánamo detainees, was unable to respond personally Tuesday because he was on the Guantánamo-bound flight.

A statement issued by his deputy, Mike Berrigan, speaks of "various professional responsibility issues" affecting Mr.

Khadr's entire Pentagon-appointed defence team—which comprises four attorneys including Lt.-Cmdr. Kuebler.

"No detailed defence counsel, including Lt.-Cmdr. Kuebler and the three other defence counsel detailed to defend Omar Khadr, have been allowed to travel to Guantánamo the last two weeks pending the resolution of these ethical issues on the Khadr trial defence team," the statement says.

"Col. Masciola made this decision in fairness to all defence counsel involved and in the best interest of the effective representation of Omar Khadr."

A Conflict of Interest?

Mr. Berrigan said in an e-mail exchange he could not go into detail about the "ethical issues" he mentioned in his statement "given the nature of the issues and the status of the investigation."

But in his statement, he denies Col. Masciola is involved in any conflict of interest.

"Lt.-Cmdr. Kuebler has raised certain allegations against the chief defence counsel to the chief defence counsel's supervisor," the statement says. "Those allegations will no doubt be dealt with in an appropriate manner in due course."

One outcome could be that the military commission system established by the former [George W.] Bush administration in the wake of the Sept. 11, 2001, attacks will be abandoned—thereby throwing into question the future of both Col. Masciola's office, and that of the military prosecutors, within the Office of Military Commission.

However, the defence counsel section could survive if the same military lawyers were allowed to represent the detainees in U.S. federal courts.

"I believe Omar should be repatriated to Canada, and not put through a federal court," Lt.-Cmdr. Kuebler said. "Since that is the position of Omar's defence attorney, no one on the defence side should be trying to shift his case to a federal court."

Lt.-Cmdr. Kuebler says in his news release that Col. Masciola "refused to answer" e-mails sent Saturday and Monday "seeking to determine whether he has a conflict."

An Inquiry Is Launched

The release says the order barring Lt.-Cmdr. Kuebler from the Guantánamo-bound flight came down Monday afternoon. By that time, the release adds, Lt.-Cmdr. Kuebler had told Col. Masciola he intended to "take the matter up" with Col. Masciola's supervisor.

Lt.-Cmdr. Kuebler also highlights Col. Masciola has launched an inquiry into the entire row—but says it is headed by an officer who works for the chief.

"This is tantamount to Col. Masciola investigating himself," Lt.-Cmdr. Kuebler's release says.

Since he is unable to meet with Mr. Khadr, Lt.-Cmdr. Kuebler said he has effectively been "prohibited from disclosing information about the matter" to him.

His release adds he "raised concerns about a potential conflict of interest driving Col. Masciola's management decisions on several occasions over the past few weeks."

In turn, "Masciola [expressed] concerns about Lt.-Cmdr. Kuebler's 'management' of the Khadr defence team last week," the release says.

Arrested in July 2002 following a firefight with U.S. forces in Afghanistan, Khadr faces five war crimes charges, including murder in the death of a U.S. serviceman.

The cases of all charged Guantánamo detainees are under review after President Barack Obama ordered prosecutors to ask for a suspension in proceedings.

> *"Canada can't have it both ways—it can't both exercise its own sovereign authority over its border policies, and expect the United States not to do the same thing."*

Canada's Security Policies Are Too Lax

Paul Rosenzweig

Paul Rosenzweig is the former deputy assistant secretary for policy at the US Department of Homeland Security and now works for Red Branch Consulting, a homeland security consulting firm. In the following viewpoint, he maintains that ever since the terrorist attacks of September 11, 2001, the United States has been working to tighten security at its borders. Rosenzweig claims that the United States came to see that Canada is not on the same page with security matters, and therefore the United States resolved to act in its own interests to protect its people—even if it clashed with Canadian policy.

As you read, consider the following questions:

1. On what date were Americans and Canadians crossing the border required to show passports?

Paul Rosenzweig, "Why the U.S. Doesn't Trust Canada," *Maclean's*, October 5, 2009. Reprinted with permission.

2. What broad strategic proposal did the US Department of Homeland Security make to the Canadian government in 2006?

3. Why has the Maher Arar incident eroded trust between the United States and Canada?

On June 1, [2009], for the first time in history, Canadians and Americans crossing the border were required to show a passport (or equivalent) document. By all accounts, the transition has, despite Canadian fears, proceeded with remarkably modest disruption. Canadians, however, continue to question the requirement and to object to other U.S. border security measures. As I worked (on behalf of the United States) over the past four years to prepare for these changes, most Canadians expressed a quiet dismay: "How," they wondered, "could you be doing this to us when we are such good friends?"

A Change in Policy

After all, it has been a major sea change in the American approach to the land border with Canada. For more than 100 years, though Canadians have thought frequently and almost obsessively about the United States, most Americans have paid relatively little attention to Canada. Except for those who live close to the border (let's all say it together: "the longest undefended border in the world") or whose business is linked to Canadian products, most Americans don't hold any strong opinion about Canada. You're just like us, we think, only a little different and a little less temperate. We're the lucky ones, because we have Florida (though each winter the residents of Ontario invade).

In the years since 9/11 [the September 11, 2001, terrorist attacks on the World Trade Center and the Pentagon], I think many Canadians have come to yearn for this era of benign neglect. Before then, Canada had come to rely on the fact that

America had not been paying very much attention to it. In effect, that let Canada have the best of both worlds—the capacity and interest in pursuing policies that are independent from those followed by the United States, joined with the enjoyment of an open border that substantially reduced any practical sovereign distinction between the two countries insofar as travel and trade were concerned.

The result was an undefended border, but one that had an inherent tension to it as differences grew in American and Canadian policies. By and large, Canada has much greater openness to the rest of the world than does the U.S. Canadian asylum policies are more liberal; Canada extends the privilege of visa-free travel to the citizens of many more countries. And, more fundamentally, Canada takes a much lighter hand in screening arriving travellers.

Differences in Security Practices

These are, of course, generalizations, so let me provide a specific example. The United States has long had challenges on its southern border with Mexico. At this juncture, we have fairly stringent identification requirements for Mexicans entering the United States directly. Yet until new Canadian visa restrictions came into effect on July 14 [2009], Canada had chosen to allow visa-free travel for Mexicans to Canada; the lack of a more concrete identification requirement on the part of the U.S. at the northern border until June 1 created an opportunity for Mexicans to evade the southern border restrictions. Let me be clear: Canada is a good friend of the United States and a separate sovereign nation. It is, and ought to be, perfectly free to make independent sovereign decisions regarding its admissions policies. Nobody in the United States would say otherwise. But differences—like Canada's past treatment of Mexican nationals—necessarily have consequences.

Before Sept. 11, 2001, the disharmony in immigration and border control policies was of relatively minor importance—

certainly not worth attempting to correct if the cost would be a disruption in cross-border trade. That changed after the attacks on the World Trade Center and the Pentagon. At the Department of Homeland Security (DHS), where I served, we spent a large fraction of our time thinking about Canada—and with good reason. Created in 2003, DHS is the locus for American efforts to prevent another terrorist attack on the United States. To a large degree that means that DHS is a border security agency—and as a border agency, we worry about (surprise!) borders. That means that DHS spends a lot of its time thinking about Canada (along with Mexico and our "third border" in the Caribbean), and much less time worrying about more distant overseas threats in, say, South Asia or the Middle East. For DHS, "international affairs" frequently means "Canadian affairs" (or Mexican or Caribbean).

Status Quo Is Unacceptable

So the initial problem for Canada was a simple practical one—we were paying more attention. And what we saw caused us some concern. What had earlier been very modest divergences in immigration policy now loomed larger as differences in counterterrorism policy. Some Canadians have yet to come to grips with the new reality that Canada can't have it both ways—it can't both exercise its own sovereign authority over its border policies, and expect the United States not to do the same thing. If we did we would, in effect, be outsourcing American security decisions to Canada, a state of affairs that simply cannot continue in a post-9/11 world.

This new reality would be of little moment if we had a shared sense of the terrorist problem and could anticipate a commitment to working on a convergence of policies. Unfortunately, over the course of many discussions with my Canadian colleagues, all of which have been exceedingly amiable and pleasant, I've begun to worry that the U.S. and Canada are not as closely aligned as they think they are. We have tried to work at realigning our vision (the preferred course of action), but if we don't succeed and continue down a path of divergence, that will, inevitably, lead to even greater disparities and controversies between the two countries.

The opening assumption that I brought to the negotiating table, and that I think every American would begin with, is that the U.S. and Canada more or less see the world in the same way. At the core, we like to believe that we think alike and have the same aim—a free and safe citizenry. Increasingly, however, I'm not sure this assumption holds. We don't seem to see the world the same way anymore, and as a result there is perceptible erosion in the trust between us. Americans responded to Sept. 11 in ways that most Canadians don't seem to have internalized. At an intellectual level, they recognize that 9/11 was a traumatic experience for the U.S. They understand and respect the fact that it has caused a reaction. But in their most candid moments, I suspect most Canadians think the U.S. overreacted (a view that some in the U.S.—though likely a minority—also share). Many Americans, by contrast, think that Canada didn't react enough to Sept. 11, and that what little reaction there was amounted to, if anything, tepid half measures.

Opportunities to Coordinate Efforts

Back in 2006, DHS made a broad strategic proposal to our Canadian counterparts: let's work to synchronize our perimeter security approaches as much as possible. The payoff would be relaxed controls along our mutual border. I remember when then DHS secretary Michael Chertoff first presented this idea to his counterpart, Stockwell Day, then minister for public safety. We laid out a comprehensive proposal that included: greater information sharing, coordinated standards for passenger screening, shared technology and targeting for cargo containers, and other similar concepts. Essentially, we proposed a joint security model for homeland security that resembled

NORAD [North American Aerospace Defense Command] in conception. Even at that first meeting the response from Canada was lukewarm, at best.

I continue to believe that there are many real benefits that would flow from co-operation of this sort. Here's a concrete example. The U.S. has begun to develop a series of policies aimed at deterring the importation of a nuclear weapon or radiological material for a "dirty bomb" into the United States aboard small private aircraft (known, in the trade, as "general aviation"). Some of those policies are internal to the U.S.—we'll be requiring better identification for passengers and pilots, for example. But one key component of the strategy is the idea of screening general aviation airplanes overseas, before they depart for the United States.

This was a win-win proposition for everyone. America would have greater security, since any radioactive material would be interdicted before it even started toward the U.S. The general aviation community would benefit, since they would undergo all of the regular U.S. customs and immigration screening overseas and then be allowed to travel to any airport in the U.S. (instead of the current practice, where they must first land at an official port of entry, like Miami, and then fly onward to their ultimate destination). And the host country and airport would benefit from increased traffic, with the resulting economic benefits. The attraction is so great that in less than two years the U.S. has already signed agreements of this sort with Ireland, Bermuda and Aruba. More are likely.

Early on, we saw this as a great opportunity to synchronize our perimeter security with Canada. The idea would be for Canadians to co-locate their own customs and immigration officials at the same facilities and provide the same service for Canada-bound general aviation. Since it's unlikely that a terrorist would actually be able to acquire a loose nuclear weapon in Canada, there would be no real need for screening Canadian traffic to the U.S. if Canada and U.S. radiological screening overseas were coordinated in this way.

Canada Does Not Take Terrorism Seriously Enough

I can't say why, but while I was at DHS we had absolutely no real expression of Canadian interest in the project (or in any of the other synchronization proposals). I personally briefed our general aviation plans to Canadian delegations on at least three occasions—but when I left DHS in January 2009, Canadian participation in a joint general aviation screening program was firmly placed on the back burner.

Maybe it is because the nature of minority government prevents co-operation of this sort. Maybe it was the product of a distrust of the [George W.] Bush administration that will dissipate now that Barack Obama is president. But I suspect, as well, that it simply reflects a Canadian disposition toward the terrorism issue: If you don't think terrorism is that important an issue, then you aren't willing to invest the time and energy required to address the problem. And if that really is the cause of our divergence of views, it will become a permanent and enduring reality, with consequences at the border.

Finally, there is one other piece to the puzzle that must be mentioned in any candid assessment of the U.S.-Canada relationship. Since both countries, broadly speaking, seek the same social ends through the same governmental means, we have come to believe that we each are a trustworthy partner. There is a very good, historical basis for this trust. We used to say at DHS: "If the Canadians say they will do something, they'll do it." I'm not sure that mutual trust exists as much anymore—especially Canadian belief in American trustworthiness. Though we continue to co-operate closely and well on a tactical level (shared law enforcement investigations and the like), I and my colleagues at more senior levels had a distinct perception of distancing by our Canadian counterparts, and a notable reduction in our ability to share information across the border.

The Repercussions of the Arar Incident

Much of this, I think, traces back to the Maher Arar [a Canadian Syrian citizen deported by the United States to Syria where he was allegedly tortured] incident. And here I begin to worry even more, because I cannot see reconciliation. In Canada, the belief is that Arar was mistreated. It has become so strong a belief that it has become an article of faith. This is neither the time nor the place to rehash the questions about Arar, save to make an important point that often gets lost: The U.S. is both entitled to, and obliged to, form its own judgment about Arar.

And reasonable friends may interpret facts differently. Where Canadians see an innocent 20-minute walk in the rain (according to the report issued by Justice Dennis O'Connor, who oversaw Canada's public inquiry into the affair, on Oct. 11, 2001, Arar spent 20 minutes outside in the rain talking to an individual who was the subject of an ongoing terrorism investigation), some Americans (and the RCMP [Royal Canadian Mounted Police]) see behaviour reminiscent of those seeking to avoid surveillance and "taking great pains not to be overheard." A walk in the rain is, in our experience, a tactic frequently adopted by organized crime figures to avoid audio surveillance. On the basis of this conduct, and other information, I expect that Arar will continue to remain an object of U.S. concern for the indefinite future.

This is not to say that either side is necessarily right in its judgment about Arar's activity, and it is certainly not to suggest that what Arar reports having experienced in Syria was proper treatment. But it is to say that the Canadian reaction to what is, at worst, a disagreement as to a single (albeit prominent) case does broad damage to our relationship—and that damage can have wide-ranging effects. If we do not trust each other enough, we are unlikely to find ways to bring greater openness to our borders.

An Erosion of Trust

But another aspect of the erosion of trust, from our side of the border, lay in Canadian public diplomacy over the potential imposition of border controls. What would be the reaction in Canada if American cabinet officials and ambassadors were personally engaged in overt efforts to lobby Parliament to change Canadian laws that Americans thought were not beneficial? Canadians would, and quite rightly, object. Yet, for nearly four years, I witnessed exactly congruent Canadian conduct—ministers and your ambassador vigorously lobbying Congress for a change in American law. On at least one occasion, the ambassador hosted a dinner at the embassy for the sole apparent purpose of having all of his guests publicly lecture the DHS officials present about how wrongheaded our policies were. Discussions that ought to have occurred between our respective executive branches were made the fodder of American politics. And that, too, erodes trust.

Indeed, given the successful implementation of the passport requirement—which by most accounts has had a modest disruptive effect on trade and travel—we can see, in retrospect, how Canadian fears caused Canadians to overreact. There is a bit of an irony here, because overreaction is supposed to be the flaw in America's response to the terrorism threat, not the flaw in Canada's response to America.

There is still much to be celebrated in our relationship. Despite our differences, we continue to co-operate routinely in ways that no two other countries in the world are capable of doing. But that kind of relationship requires constant care and attention. For too long we've benefited from a lack of any challenges. Today that is changing—we have much work to do to rebuild a shared consensus and world view and recreate an atmosphere of trust. The task is not an easy one, and the first step on the road is a candid assessment of where we are. No longer can we rely on just hoping we don't notice our differences. Instead, let's begin to acknowledge them for what they are, with the hope and expectation that good friends can resolve them if they are willing.

> "America will remain Canada's biggest
> opportunity, and greatest challenge, for
> years to come."

America's Security Policies
Are Too Stringent

Luiza Ch. Savage with John Geddes

Luiza Ch. Savage is the US correspondent and a blogger for
Maclean's, *a Canadian national weekly current affairs magazine, and John Geddes is the Ottawa bureau chief for* Maclean's.
*In the following viewpoint, they argue that in addition to secu-
rity problems between the United States and Canada, there is
also growing tension over America's protectionist trade policies
and myriad other issues. Savage and Geddes explore recent attempts to find common ground as well as opportunities to cooperate on border and security issues.*

As you read, consider the following questions:

1. What country did Stephen Harper compare Canada to
   in 2007 to provide insight into its worsening relationship with the United States?

2. How was the NHL affected by tightened US security
   policies in 2009?

Luiza Ch. Savage, "Canada's Biggest Problem? America," *Maclean's*, October 7, 2009.
Reprinted with permission.

3. What is an example that Savage and Geddes give of US-Canada cooperation?

It has been almost two years since Stephen Harper disclosed that his cabinet was having serious discussions about what to do to "restore the special Canadian and American relationship" that he said had become "lost" in the [George W.] Bush years. "What has happened is that Canada lost that special relationship with the United States. We increasingly became viewed as just another foreign country, albeit an ally, a good friend, but nevertheless a foreign country. You know, the northern equivalent of Mexico in terms of the border," the Prime Minister told *Maclean's* in an interview back in December 2007. "That isn't just a shift in the view of the administration, that's somewhat a shift in American public opinion as well, which concerns me."

At the time, Harper was preoccupied with a new passport requirement that threatened tourism and trade, adding a new scale to the ongoing red-tape "thickening" of the world's longest undefended border. "I'm certain this trend will not be reversed in the lifetime of the current American administration," Harper said at the time. "I'm more optimistic it will be deferred later by a new administration." But, he added, "I'm far from sure."

The "Special Relationship" Is in Trouble

He was right to be wary. If the special relationship was lost under George W. Bush, nine months into the new administration it remains missing. At his Sept. 16 [2009] meeting with [Barack] Obama at the White House, Harper boasted that it was his seventh session with the new president. But the passport requirement remains, as do agricultural inspection fees on commercial cross-border traffic and air travellers. Instead of "unthickening" the border, the new administration has kept the Bush policies in place and even piled more on: In February, the U.S. sent unmanned aerial surveillance drones to patrol parts of the border with Canada. The drones, which can detect human movement 10 km [kilometers] away, are supposed to help catch smugglers. But they have raised concerns about privacy in border communities, and although they are unarmed, give the 49th parallel something in common with the tribal lands between Afghanistan and Pakistan.

Since Obama's February [2009] trip to Ottawa, where he was greeted with a rapturous welcome on his first official foreign visit, the state of the world's largest trading relationship has become even more fraught. Given that fully one-quarter of the Canadian economy depends on exports to the U.S., growing American protectionism has proven to be a growing threat. Problems began with a Buy American provision in the US$787-billion stimulus bill. While there have been reports that an exemption for Canada may be imminent, in return for Canadian municipal and provincial governments allowing procurement contracts for U.S. companies, rules similar to the Buy American provision are now being repeated in other legislation. Protectionism has also surfaced in proposed climate change legislation that would impose border tariffs on imports from countries whose carbon policies Washington deems insufficient. And there are other issues galore that affect Canada, from complicated and costly trucking rules and the treatment of Canadian hydroelectricity under U.S. environmental laws to "country of origin" labelling that imposes costs on Canadian agricultural producers and reduces the appeal of their goods in the U.S. marketplace.

The NHL Problems

Oh—there's Canada's national sport as well. In August [2009], Canadian NHL [National Hockey League] teams faced the prospect of having their seasons thrown into limbo by a sudden Obama administration crackdown on Canadian charter flights operating between U.S. cities. That issue arose when a

"Stop Canadian terrorist beaver!" Cartoon by Sneuro. www.CartoonStock.com.

U.S. charter airline and an American pilots' union complained that the Air Canada charter company was beginning to take U.S. business, and the Department of Transportation stepped in. When Harper sat down with Obama at his Sept. 16 Oval Office meeting, he took precious minutes away from discussions of Afghanistan and Iran to address the war over hockey players.

That problem was eventually resolved, with Air Canada agreeing to "an unprecedented level of monitoring and enforcement" of who boards the flights. But it was just one more high-profile imbroglio between the two countries that may have left many Canadians asking the question: Is America Canada's biggest problem?

American Protectionism on the Rise

Jason Myers, the president of the Canadian Manufacturers & Exporters, calls growing American protectionism "the hottest issue for us." He is not only concerned about new rules that affect us directly, but also those aimed at other countries that lead to problems for Canada. For example, when Obama announced in September that the U.S. would impose tariffs on tires from China, Myers worried that any Chinese retaliation against the U.S. auto industry would hurt Canadian businesses, too, because that sector is so integrated in North America. "We just see a whole lot of areas where the U.S. is becoming more closed, protectionist and isolated in terms of trade," Myers says. "It's not just that it's our biggest market, but we make things together. We are part of an integrated supply chain. It has far-reaching impacts throughout industries."

The impact of the Buy American provisions has been not only to exclude Canadian suppliers from government contracts at the state and local level, but also to encourage American distributors to stop carrying Canadian products. "The impact of this goes well beyond the procurement markets at state and local levels and beyond the federal restrictions," Myers says. The economic impact is hard to estimate, in part because only a small portion of the stimulus money has been disbursed, but at least 250 Canadian companies have lost business, he adds.

Washington, Ottawa and the provinces have worked toward a solution to the problem. But even if Canada gains an exemption from the Buy American provision, Canadian businesses are worried that initiative may have been just the tip of the iceberg. Similar protectionist rules have been included in several bills pending in Congress, including the Water Quality Investment Act, which Myers notes could affect $4 billion worth of Canadian exports.

Conflict Rooted in Economics

Of course, U.S. protectionism is rising precisely because the American economy is struggling, with the country's global trade deficit now a domestic political football. To American ears, this drumbeat of Canadian complaints is beginning to look predatory. The Canadian Embassy arms itself with fancy maps detailing just how many jobs in each congressional district depend on the annual US$742 billion in trade with Canada. But congressmen know a trade deficit when they see one: The Canada-U.S. imbalance happens to amount to several billion dollars each month—in Canada's favour (it was US$2.2 billion in July).

"I think we need a whole new vocabulary in the relationship," says Scotty Greenwood, executive director of the Washington-based Canadian American Business Council. The two countries are often tone-deaf to each other's politics, she observes. "Canadians like to talk about NAFTA [North American Free Trade Agreement] and say, 'We're your biggest trading relationship.' Well, here NAFTA is a dirty word and everyone knows that Canada has a trade surplus. That is not what Americans want to hear. Basically, Canada is saying, you guys are an awesome market. We know that. We want you to be an awesome market for us, too."

Understanding U.S. Security Concerns

Likewise, in an America where national security concerns are top of mind, Canadian complaints about "thickening" at the border fall on deaf ears, Greenwood says, including those of the new secretary of homeland security. "Janet Napolitano leaned over to me at a dinner," she recalls, "and said, 'They talk about this like it's a bad thing.'" Greenwood suggests new language for discussing border issues. "The Canadian vocabulary should be something like, 'smart, breathable armour.' If Canadians would talk about it as smart, breathable armour it would automatically reassure Americans that you understand the concerns." Canadian governments should adapt to the fact that U.S. attitudes changed permanently after 9/11 [the September 11, 2001, terrorist attacks on the United States], she says. "It's like the passport thing. If you want Canadians to be advantaged and have privileged access to the U.S., then get a secure card instead of arguing that we should accept 5,000 different documents."

David Wilkins, the former U.S. ambassador to Canada, says Canadians should recognize the immense power of Congress when trying to press their case. That is what Wilkins himself is doing in his new role as a lobbyist for Saskatchewan, which wants to develop and export production from its oil sands at a time when some members of Congress want to penalize "dirty oil" in upcoming climate change legislation. He recently flew several influential U.S. senators to the province to see a joint Canadian-American carbon capture and sequestration project aimed at reducing greenhouse gas emissions. He also praised Harper for calling on congressional leaders on Capitol Hill during his last visit to Washington. "He obviously gets it because he did that visit to the Hill," says Wilkins.

Better late than never, says Colin Robertson, a former Canadian diplomat in Washington. "It's been five years since a Canadian prime minister has been out there in a formal sense," says Robertson, a senior fellow at the Norman Paterson School of International Affairs at Carleton University. "It is entirely appropriate for the prime minister to go to Congress—he is our legislator-in-chief. If we started doing that on a consistent basis, that will give us more credibility. It opens the conversation on future engagement," he adds.

Educating the U.S. Congress

To address concerns about border security, Robertson says the heads of Canadian security agencies such as CSIS [Canadian Security Intelligence Service] and the RCMP [Royal Canadian Mounted Police], and their U.S. counterparts, should jointly educate members of Congress about the deep bilateral co-operation in law enforcement and intelligence. "If you send that information to Congress, it will make it easier on border issues," he says. Likewise, Robertson says Canadian labour should take an aggressive role in pressing top U.S. labour leaders on protectionism that hurts Canadian unions. "A third of Canadian unions are affiliates of U.S. unions. It's brother hurting brother," he says.

"Canadians need to work the American system the way the Americans themselves use it. You have to play by American rules," Myers agrees. "It's clear Canada won't go far just by trying to encourage the U.S. to do us favours," he says. "We have a lot of work to do to build a stronger voice among stakeholder groups like business associations and labour associations across Canada and the U.S. to say that we are in this together."

The International Picture

But when it comes to direct dealings with the Obama administration, Canada has to walk a fine line between raising bilateral issues and trivializing the relationship. "Because of the U.S.'s position in the world, the president is dealing with international issues, whether it's Afghanistan, Iran or North Korea," Wilkins says. "Those are the primary focus. It behooves any country dealing with the U.S. to talk about the international issues before you turn your attention to wait times at the Peace Bridge."

Robertson has much the same message. "With the Americans we tend to focus on just the little neighborhood stuff," he complains, noting that the Canadian emphasis on bilateral irritants came to irritate Bush's secretary of state, Condoleezza Rice. "She would say, 'Here come the Canadians with their condominium issues.'" Robertson, for one, regrets that Harper raised the issue of hockey flights at his tête-à-tête with Obama, rather than leaving it to ministers and ambassadors. "It makes them wonder: Are we dealing with a border state governor or a serious G8 [Group of Eight forum for the governments of the world's major economies] nation? We tend to ratchet stuff up because we think this is what the public wants. But the public wants results. A lot of stuff the president can't resolve."

Meanwhile, Robertson says, the U.S. is strongly interested in the Canadian perspective and Canadian contacts on issues from Afghanistan to Pakistan to the Western Hemisphere. Indeed, the outgoing Canadian ambassador to Washington, Michael Wilson, has called Canada's military role in Afghanistan the "best calling card I had" in Washington. When that military commitment winds down, it will not make the Canada-U.S. relationship any easier. "That's going to be front and centre for the government, for Parliament, for some time, as to how we handle this in a way that doesn't undermine the terrific goodwill that we have," he told *Maclean's* in a recent interview.

Opportunities for Cooperation

Despite the tensions, there have been notable examples of smooth co-operation between the two countries on urgent matters. Facing a possible swine flu pandemic, labs in Canada, the U.S. and Mexico worked together to identify the new virus. There were also the neatly dovetailed government bailouts for the auto industry. "It was definitely a team effort," says Ann-Marie McGaughey, a partner at the law firm McKenna Long & Aldridge, who was counsel for the Canadian government in the negotiations. "The word at the top was 'get it done,' and everybody tried to find a way to make it happen." Despite the Canadian government's much smaller stake in Chrysler and General Motors, McGaughey says that "from the beginning the mantra was, 'U.S. and Canada side by side.' Which meant if it was a right or a privilege that the U.S. was getting, then Canada would get it too."

Lawrence Cannon, Canada's foreign affairs minister, says that while border thickening and Buy American issues draw disproportionate attention, the underlying relationship is solid. "They aren't issues that prevent us from continuing on a good relationship," he says. Evidence that the Conservative government is working on the bilateral bonds can be found in the 36 trips by Canadian cabinet ministers to Washington since Obama took office, as well as the eight meetings between the prime minister and the president (the last one was at the G-20 [Group of Twenty summit] in Pittsburgh). Obama, too, has tried to put a happy face on relations. At his meeting with Harper on Sept. 16 [2009], he said protectionism is a "legitimate issue" but encouraged Canadians "to keep things in perspective." "Canada continues to be a huge trading partner to the United States," the president added. "Businesses in the United States and Canada both benefit from that trade, as do consumers. On the scale of our overall trading relationship, [irritants] shouldn't be considered the dominant element of our economic relationship."

Developing Other Relationships

But Liberal MP [Member of Parliament] Scott Brison, his party's trade critic, says the Tories started out with a serious disadvantage when Obama came into power, since Harper had been seen as ideologically close to Bush. "Their focus was very much partisan and ideological," Brison charges. He slams the Harper government for failing to adequately push back against new border rules that have decreased casual travel between the two countries, which he says has been "devastating" for Canadian small businesses that rely on U.S. travellers. Brison also says Ottawa should have fought back harder against new U.S. country-of-origin labelling rules that hurt Canadian food producers.

And there is a growing recognition in Ottawa that Canada can't count on things getting better quickly. In the halls of the Foreign Affairs and International Trade Department there's growing talk of diversifying to other countries as a hedge against not-so-reliable U.S. markets. Trade Minister Stockwell Day alluded to that during a recent two-day mission to Brazil to promote trade and investment. "We do have a relationship with the U.S. that is in many ways the envy of the world," Day said. "But as we have experienced, when they hit a downturn in the economy, their demand drops and that hits us hard." Brazil, which has emerged as the clear focal point of Ottawa's beyond-the-U.S.A. strategy in the Western Hemisphere, is a huge prize—an economy just slightly smaller than Canada's and a notch bigger than Mexico's. Day, in fact, has been to Brazil twice since being named trade minister after last fall's election. In 2008, Canadian exports to Brazil—everything from fertilizer to paper—totalled $2.6 billion, a 70 per cent leap over the previous year. "We see our engagement with Brazil kicking up to a new strategic level as a partner in the post-economic-crisis global marketplace," said one Canadian trade official.

That may be so. But America will remain Canada's biggest opportunity, and greatest challenge, for years to come. After all, Brazil remains small potatoes compared to the U.S. market. And there is nowhere else for those NHL charter flights to go.

| "In Canada, we have a social and eco-
logical responsibility to be water guardians by defending and protecting the
freshwater systems that lie north of the
49th parallel."

Canada Should Protect Its Water from the United States

Tony Clarke

*Tony Clarke is the founder and director of the Polaris Institute
and the author of several books on water policy. In the following
viewpoint, he underscores the importance of protecting Canada's
water resources against the encroachment of the US government
but expresses doubts that the current Canadian administration
can be a strong leader on the issue.*

As you read, consider the following questions:

1. How far back have Canadians had concerns that the United States is coming after their water supply?

2. What percentage of America's large cities are expected to face serious water shortages by 2015?

Tony Clarke, "Turning on Canada's Tap? Why We Need a Pan Canadian Policy and
Strategy Now on Bulk Water Exports to the US," Polaris Institute, April 2008, pp. 1–5.
Reprinted with permission.

3. According to the World Resources Institute, where does Canada rank in the world in terms of renewable water supply?

Prime Minister Stephen Harper had promised Canadians in the last Throne Speech [October 21, 2007] that his government would bring forth a 'national water strategy.' But the Harper Government's budget of February 26, 2008, contained no provisions for a federal water program and strategy. Meanwhile, the prospects of bulk water exports to the United States continue to be a hot policy issue simmering just below the surface on Parliament Hill.

In April 2007, people in Canada awoke to news reports that "water transfers" to the U.S. were on the agenda of a closed door meeting in Calgary of the North American Future 2025 Project—an officially sanctioned body of high-level business personnel established to advise the political leaders of Canada, Mexico and the U.S. on agenda items to be dealt with under their Security and Prosperity Partnership [of North America (SPP)]. Highlighting the emerging problems of water scarcity in the U.S. [and also Mexico], the business advisors proposed the option of developing regional agreements "on issues such as water consumption, water transfers, artificial divisions of freshwater. . . ." Less than two months later, the House of Commons voted 134 to 108 on a resolution, June 5, 2007, calling on the federal government to "quickly begin talks with its American and Mexican counterparts to exclude water from the scope of NAFTA [North American Free Trade Agreement]."

Historically speaking, there is nothing new about this public policy debate. For half a century or more, people in Canada have expressed fears that the U.S. is coming after 'our water.' In the early 1960s, public opposition to large-scale water exports to the U.S. erupted when it became known that private companies were developing plans for massive water diversion projects like the North American Water and Power [Alliance] and the GRAND Canal [Great Recycling and Northern Development Canal]. Two decades later, public anxiety about bulk water exports surfaced again during the Inquiry on a National Water Policy which, in 1985, set the stage for the Canada Water Preservation bill in 1987, effectively banning bulk water exports. Ironically, however, the proposed water legislation died on the order paper with the dissolution of Parliament for the 1988 election on free trade.

Under the U.S. presidency of George W. Bush, the issue has taken on a unique twist of its own. Shortly after he was sworn into office, President Bush spoke to reporters about the growing problems of water scarcity in his home state of Texas and announced he would take up the issue with then Prime Minister Jean Chrétien. While Canadian officials were quick to publicly reject Bush's overture, the signal had been given. Throughout the Bush administration, this signal has been kept alive, notably by the previous U.S. ambassador to Canada, Paul Cellucci, who gently but constantly chided Canadians in speeches about their public attitudes towards water which, from his perspective, should be viewed as another commodity like oil to be sold and exported.

In Canada, we have a social and ecological responsibility to be water guardians by defending and protecting the freshwater systems that lie north of the 49th parallel. However, it is highly doubtful that the Harper government or, for that matter any federal government, is going to take the kind of bold leadership required on this issue, without a great deal of public pressure from people across the country.

America's Water Crisis

In Canada these days, there tends to be a fair amount of loose talk about the U.S. water crisis. While water shortages certainly exist here and there across the U.S., in some cases very serious ones, it's important to probe a little deeper. When it comes to water supplies, for instance, people in this country may be surprised to learn that the U.S. is one of the most endowed countries on the planet. Here, we are not talking about surface water supplies like lakes but, more importantly, renewable water supplies which have to do with the amount of water flows and groundwater recharge that exists within the borders of a given country. In terms of renewable water supplies, the U.S. is ranked fourth in the world, one-tenth of a percentage point behind Canada.

To grasp the realities of the looming U.S. water crisis, we need to look at how urban and regional demands for water are outstripping local sources and supplies. In the U.S. today, the vast majority of the population—almost 80 percent—live in cities and the watersheds of the American city are depleting. Surveys are showing that in an increasing number of cities, there are signs that the traditional water sources which urban areas depend on are either drying up or becoming so contaminated that new water sources have to be found. According to the Urban Water Council, 24 percent of America's medium-sized cities and 17.3 percent of its large cities are expected to face serious water shortages by 2015.

A Regional Analysis

The problem of U.S. water shortages becomes even more disturbing when viewed on a region-by-region basis. In particular, there are three major regions of rapidly growing water shortages.

Southwest States: The fastest growing region in the U.S. is already dry and must pump water in from elsewhere. In Arizona, the city of Tucson has part of its water supplies pumped in from the Colorado [River] while in the city of Phoenix, which is growing at a rate of one acre per hour, water tables have reportedly dropped by as much as 120 metres in the eastern section. In California, the water table under the San Joaquin Valley has dropped nearly ten metres in some areas in the past fifty years while overuse of groundwater in the Central Valley has resulted in a loss of over 40 percent of the storage capacity in California's reservoirs. Similar trends show water shortages are intensifying in New Mexico, Texas, Nevada and Utah.

Midwest States: The farm belt of the U.S. faces a lethal combination of droughts and dried up wells. Here, the Ogallala [or High Plains] Aquifer located under some eight states, the largest single underground body of water or aquifer in all of North America, which irrigates 8.2 million acres of farm land, is being drained at a rate that is 14 times faster than nature can restore it. Half the Ogallala water is now gone. In metro Chicago, studies now warn that water demands will rise another 30 percent by 2025, thereby requiring a major escalation of bulk water transfers from Lake Michigan. And, in 2004, half of Kentucky's 120 counties had water shortages.

Southeast States: [These states] continue to encounter growing water shortages. The Florida aquifer system, which covers some 200,000 square kilometres, is currently being mined at a rate that is far faster than it can be naturally replenished. Indeed, the water table has dropped so low in Florida that seawater is now said to be invading its aquifers. Recently plagued by periodic droughts, a 'water war' is emerging in the region as Florida, Alabama, and Georgia struggle for access to, and control over, limited water supplies. As the city of Atlanta runs out of drinking water and turns to sources like the Tennessee River to solve its problems, neighboring states are vigorously objecting to these kinds of inter-basin transfers.

To be sure, significant progress has been made in water conservation. Over the last 25 years, many U.S. states and cities have begun to introduce programs and measures designed to encourage conservation pricing, conjunctive use of ground and surface water, wastewater recycling, rainwater harvesting, drip irrigation, and leak reduction methods. But, this is not enough to stem the tide.

Canada Has No Water to Spare

The conservationist argument disputes the widespread notion propagated by the export lobby that Canada has an overabundance of water. The recurrent line is that Canada, with just half of one per cent of the world's population, holds fully one-quarter of the world's fresh-water supply and, therefore, has as much to share as can profitably be moved.

But of that, only over six per cent is actually renewable, making Canada fairly average by global standards, and the greater part of that flows in relatively inaccessible northern rivers. Furthermore, less than three per cent of that renewable supply is handy to the Canada-U.S. border, where most Canadians live. While these would be the most economically viable waters to tap for bulk export, they are already being used to capacity or toxically polluted and additional major withdrawals would have devastating effects on the ecosystems they sustain.

Montreal Gazette,
"Should We Sell Our Water to the U.S.?"
November 27, 2008.

Canadian Water Sources

In the eyes of most Americans, Canada is seen as that "great, green sponge" up-North. Most maps of Canada are dotted with blotches of blue, marking numerous interconnected lakes and rivers. Yet, the topography of this country is such that we have a few very large lakes combined with a great many small lakes and, given a relatively cool climate, there is also a low rate of evaporation. Moreover, even being endowed with many lakes and rivers does not mean that Canada has a rich abundant supply of available freshwater.

Although Canada may contain as much as 20 percent of the world's lake water, this is not the same as renewable supplies of water. If water is continuously drained from a lake, it will eventually dry up. Lake water, in other words, is essentially nonrenewable. However, renewable supply is water that falls from the sky in the form of rain and snow, and then runs off in rivers, streams and underground aquifers. It also includes groundwater because, as rainfall water seeps into the ground filling up aquifers, the excess water is drained through springs which run into streams.

According to the World Resources Institute, Canada is ranked third in the world in terms of renewable water supply with 6.5 percent [behind Brazil at 12.4 and Russia at 10 percent]. Actually, Canada is virtually in a tie with three other countries—Indonesia, the U.S., and China—each with 6.4 percent of renewable water supplies. But, Canada's 6.5 percent of renewable water is also misleading. Approximately, 60 percent of this country's rivers flow northward into the Arctic and northern territories, away from where the vast majority of Canadians live and work.

As a result, it is estimated that Canada's real portion of the world's freshwater supplies is 2.6 rather than 6.5 percent. The U.S., therefore, has around 2 ½ times the amount of renewable freshwater supplies as Canada for most of its population. And, even when the Alaskan portion of the total U.S. freshwater supply is excluded, the 48 contiguous states of the mainland still have 1 ½ times the amount of renewable freshwater as does the southern half of Canada. Of course, this renewable water supply is for animal and plant life as well as human use. What's more, the U.S. population is nearly 10 times that of Canada. On top of this, scientists are warning that global warming will have a significant impact in reducing Canada's supplies of renewable freshwater. According to recent University of Alberta studies, the Prairies are already drying up: the South Saskatchewan River has declined 80 percent, the Old

Man and Peace Rivers are down 40 percent, while the Athabasca River has dropped by 30 percent. What's more, a glacier meltdown due to global warming will most certainly accelerate these trends. Meanwhile, Canada's wetlands, which play a vital role in the regeneration of freshwater, are vanishing at an alarming rate. Almost a decade ago, the Canadian Wildlife Federation warned that Canada's wetlands, which have traditionally covered only 14 percent of this country's land mass, have been mostly destroyed by urban sprawl and large-scale farming.

Moreover, when it comes to the prospect of bulk water exports, there are mounting concerns about the ecological dangers of large-scale extractions from water basins. To date, there is sufficient evidence that draining massive amounts of water from lake and river basins disrupts local ecosystems, damages natural habitat, reduces biodiversity, and dries up aquifers and underground water systems. During inter-basin transfers, parasites, bacteria, viruses, fish and plants from one water body would be carried into another. Mercury contamination from the flooding required for water diversions would bio-accumulate in the tissues of mammals, thereby having damaging effects along the food chain. Large-scale structures required for the storage of exported water would also disrupt ecosystems in remote areas.

In short, Canada's reputation as a water-rich nation is somewhat misleading and bears rethinking in the light of mounting U.S. freshwater demands. Unbeknownst to most people, for example, vast amounts of water are diverted from the Hudson Bay basin into Lake Superior, by two hydro dams [the Ogoki and Long Lac], in order to compensate for water diverted through the Chicago canal to Lake Mississippi. At the same time, the growing water stress on the ecosystem south of the border is bound to have its own impacts on Canada's water sources.

Water Export Corridors

The idea of selling Canadian water to the U.S. is certainly not new. The call for bulk water exports from Canada to the U.S. dates back to the 1960s. It is often forgotten that the precedent for bulk water exports was set back then with the signing of the Columbia River Treaty between Canada and the U.S in 1969.

Indeed, the origins of the Columbia River Treaty date back to a conflict between Arizona and California over water takings from the Colorado River which, in turn, prompted the 1963 U.S. Supreme Court ruling that a limit be placed on the volume of water withdrawals from the Colorado. Later, the void was filled by water flows from the Columbia. For almost forty years now, the Columbia River, which originates in British Columbia and is fed by water runoffs from the Rocky Mountains, has been providing the American southwest with a steady supply of water from Canada.

In order to offset its impending water shortage crisis today, the U.S. has at least two major options within its own borders. One is to tap the Great Lakes for bulk water diversion, namely, Lake Michigan [the only one of the five within U.S. borders], which would call for an expansion of the Chicago Diversion Plan originally grandfathered into the Boundary Waters Treaty between Canada and the U.S. The other option is to transport water from Alaska either by supertankers down the treacherous waterways of the Pacific Northwest coast or through an undersea pipeline along the Pacific shoreline.

Since the International Joint Commission has firmly rejected any further bulk water diversions from Great Lakes and the Alaska option may prove to be too costly or unpredictable, there is the third option of Canadian bulk water exports. Since the 1960s, three mega-water corridor plans have been promoted.

Western Corridor: Originally, the North American Water and Power Alliance [NAWAPA] was designed to bring bulk water from Alaska and northern British Columbia for delivery to 35 U.S. states. By building a series of large dams, the northward flow of the Yukon, Peace, Liard and a host of other rivers would be reversed to move southward and pumped into the Rocky Mountain Trench where the water would be trapped in a giant reservoir and then pumped through a canal transporting the water southward into Washington State and 34 other states.

Central Corridor: A set of water diversion schemes, named the Central North American Water Project [CeNAWAP], calls for a series of canals and pumping stations linking Great Bear Lake and Great Slave Lake in the NWT [Northwest Territories] to Lake Athabasca and Lake Winnipeg and then the Great Lakes for bulk water exports to the U.S. There are several variations of the CeNAWAP linking various rivers for the same ends, such is the Kuiper Diversion Scheme and the Magnum Diversion Project diverting water though similar river systems into the Souris River in the U.S.

Eastern Corridor: Known as the GRAND Canal scheme, plans called for the damming and rerouting of northern river systems in Quebec in order to bring freshwater through canals down into the Great Lakes where it would be flushed into the American Midwest and the Sunbelt states. A dike would be built across James Bay at the mouth of Hudson Bay [whose natural flow is northward], thereby turning the bay into a giant freshwater reservoir fed by the 20 rivers that flow into it.

At the time, there was strong public opposition in Canada to these bulk water export schemes. Yet, there was also political support. The GRAND Canal scheme, for example, enjoyed the backing of then Quebec Premier Robert Bourassa and then Prime Minister Brian Mulroney. Even so, neither of these mega projects has come to pass. The reasons include lingering problems over their economic feasibility, conflicting political jurisdictions and disturbing environmental impacts. But, none of these massive water diversion and export schemes could be realized unless the U.S. demand and thirst was acute enough. That picture, as we have seen, is now changing dramatically.

> "Let's give ourselves a shake here: There is virtually no likelihood that the U.S. will suddenly decide to twist our tap and drain us dry."

Canada Should Share Its Water with the United States

Chris Wood

Chris Wood is a reporter and the author of Dry Spring: The Coming Water Crisis of North America. *In the following viewpoint, excerpted from his book, he asserts that Canada should take the opportunity to sell a portion of its abundant freshwater supply to the United States under the right circumstances. Wood argues that cooperation on this issue will benefit both Canadians and Americans.*

As you read, consider the following questions:

1. How does Peter Lougheed believe the United States will justify taking Canada's water?

2. How much Milk River, Alberta, water is transported through pipeline to Sweetgrass, Montana, every month?

3. What is one of the solutions Wood offers to help conserve the freshwater we do have now?

Chris Wood, "The Case for Selling Our Water," TheTyee.ca, June 12, 2008. Reprinted with permission.

We Canadians are damn serious about "our" water.

It's a source of pride for a national ego otherwise notoriously wracked by doubt. You could fit our population into greater Tokyo with futons to spare, our economy barely makes it over the threshold into the G8 [Group of Eight, a forum for the governments of the world's major economies] and our undersea navy may famously be outnumbered by the toy submarines at the West Edmonton Mall.

But when it comes to water, Canada is the 800-pound gorilla on the block. Few suggestions raise our temperature faster than that we should sell any of it, especially to America.

And few beliefs are more deeply lodged in our collective subconscious than that one day Uncle Sam will insist that we do just that. That makes it a touchy topic. After one American expert spoke in favour of continental trade in water to an audience in Vancouver, he said afterward, only partly in jest, "I felt some need to leave the country very quickly."

Left-leaning water activists work tirelessly to inflame Canadians against this "looming threat" from next door.

Thirsting for Our Water

"Canada is under pressure to sell water to the United States by pipeline or diversion," insists the Council of Canadians on its website.

The drumbeat that *the Americans are coming* for Canada's water crosses most of Canada's political divides. Peter Lougheed, the famously level-headed former premier of Alberta who helped to negotiate free trade with the United States, also believes that, "at some stage of the game, Washington is going to interpret the free trade agreement and think they have a claim over our freshwater. It's coming."

When it does, "Canadians should be prepared to respond firmly with a forceful, 'No, we need it for ourselves.'"

Even the generally pro-American and pro-market Alberta pundits Barry Cooper and David Bercuson have characterized any future dealings with the United States over water in terms of a mugging.

Water to Share

Let's give ourselves a shake here: There is virtually no likelihood that the U.S. will suddenly decide to twist our tap and drain us dry.

And despite that general truth, should a few local opportunities arise here and there to sell modest quantities of water to Americans, doing so wouldn't trigger the kind of continental demand for every drop of our water that activists invoke.

Our water has in fact flowed south by truck and pipeline for years, and yet no stampede of NAFTA [North American Free Trade Agreement]-quoting claimants has appeared at the border demanding to stick a pipe in Lake Athabasca.

There's more. If Americans or others do arrive at Canada's door with checkbooks and empty billycans, we shouldn't send them away.

Not because they might be armed and desperate. But because the water that used to fall on other lands now falls on ours; because we can spare a little in ways that won't harm our environment (and that certainly make more ecological sense than pumping it into the ground to push out oil); and yes, because we can make money by doing so.

For proof that a little buying and selling of water over the border won't bring down the sky, you need to get out of committee rooms and let the Alberta wind ruffle your hair.

Sale or No Sale?

For more than 40 years, beneath the sagebrush that surrounds the hamlet of Coutts, Alberta, a pipeline has carried water withdrawn from the Alberta reach of the Milk River south to the Americans of Sweetgrass, Montana.

In a typical month, 3,600 cubic metres flow down the pipe and over the border. In exchange, Sweetgrass's only governing body, its sewer and water board, pays Coutts roughly $4,000. Whether this constitutes a sale is a matter of interpretation.

"We buy our water from Coutts," asserts Helen van Ruden, a frank, businesslike woman in chinos and jean shirt who works at the UPS forwarding warehouse on the U.S. side. "We have for as long as I've lived here. We pay per gallon. It's been great."

Coutts Mayor Jamie Woodcock is a large fellow who staffs a much smaller UPS outpost on the Canadian side. He agrees that the arrangement works well. When Coutts had to upgrade its water treatment recently, Sweetgrass shared the cost through a hike in its water rate. But, he insists, "We don't sell it to them. We charge a fee for delivering and chlorination. We're not actually selling the water."

What the original contract may say on the point is unknown. It's been lost for years.

Water Security: A Joint Project

Water carries no passport. It is never exclusively "ours" or "theirs." Like carbon and air, it's always passing through on its way to somewhere else. For that unavoidable reason, Canadians delude ourselves in imagining that we can achieve our own water security in splendid isolation from our neighbours.

Again, the fear is not that going it alone would invite a stand-and-deliver ultimatum from a thirsty America (it wouldn't). It is simply that we will best protect the water that gives life to us both, by acting together. The price of failure to do so is written in the loose sand and blackened marshes of the former Colorado [River] Delta.

Water is a physical fact. Its challenges are always specific to the ground it flows over. Adversaries over water are usually neighbours; solutions require local compromise.

The boundaries of the conflict are typically those of the watershed, the area within which all water passes to a common outlet. Within these natural frontiers described by elevation and physics, and heedless of our invisible lines, the river course connects a single, seamless biological habitat strung out along a chain of pools from burbling beginnings to its easeful slide into the sea.

Nature's Geography

Here, every human appropriation affects every other user (human and otherwise) not only downstream but often upstream as well. If we wish to adapt to the coming storms at the least financial and ecological cost, while giving ourselves the best chance to avoid conflict, we must start here: by allowing nature's geography to trump our imaginary one in shaping not only our physical infrastructure, but our social and political infrastructures too.

Policy professionals call this idea "integrated watershed (or river basin) management."

Kindy Gosal is a policy pro with more dirty-fingernail experience than most. Raised from the age of six in the Kootenay Mountains of southeastern British Columbia, he became a forester, he says, "to get away from people."

He discovered instead that most of what threatened the health of trees came not from the forest itself but from humans. Taking this knowledge abroad, he helped communities in Africa, Tibet and Japan manage crop and forest lands more sustainably—and realized that water was the thread connecting every activity that bore on social as well as forest health in those places.

Now Gosal works with the Columbia Basin Trust, an organization funded indirectly by proceeds from the hydroelectric developments in that river basin and meant to give a stronger voice to its inhabitants.

Canada Should Sell Water to United States

- Canada has only a half percent of the world's population but it holds one-fifth of the planet's freshwater supply, half of which is renewable.

- Bulk water sales could be a lucrative source of foreign exchange for Canadians, yet the government remains firmly opposed to it.

- Pipelined water from northern Manitoba could earn the province billions a year in profits.

- An intelligent and environment-friendly water export policy could help fund Canada's stressed public health care system or, better yet, cut the country's taxes.

Frontier Centre for Public Policy,
"Water, Water Everywhere, but Canada Won't Sell It,"
September 20, 2001. www.fcpp.org.

Gosal accepts that integrated watershed management has a wonky name. But he believes deeply in its intent: to ensure that the choices we make as individuals and societies account fully for their consequences for everyone and everything else.

Bureaucratic Tangle

In the real world, that inclusive aspiration is quickly lost in the thicket of interests involved. In just the Canadian portion of the Columbia River valley, Gosal tells me, no fewer than 19 federal and 17 provincial agencies have duties that affect water, not including municipalities, First Nations and private landowners. "You have [communities with] responsibility to provide potable water," he observes, "but they can't prevent someone from putting in a pig farm."

What he calls "the essence" of integrated watershed management "is getting all the folks together who have some influence over watercourses, and the people that use the watercourse, so that you recognize what kind of activities are required to maintain the quantity and quality [of water] that we want."

The potential for conflict among fragmented authorities plagues politically divided river basins within and between nations around the world. So it is both striking and encouraging to find that in the last two decades a common desire on both sides (or ends) of these shared streams has engendered a remarkable phenomenon: new entities concerned with entire watersheds have appeared on every continent.

Even here in North America, the compelling case for managing migratory water on a watershed basis has begun to overcome American touchiness about relinquishing sovereignty to foreign agents and Canadians' reciprocal distrust of U.S. motives.

From the Rockies to the Atlantic, citizens of both nations are working to give structure and capacity to a new breed of institution that must work within, but also across, legal frontiers.

Time to Act

Yet the clock is ticking. The change in the weather—increasingly unexpected, violent, alternately drenching and desiccating—is accelerating around us. Overhead, greenhouse gases will reach the trigger point for an unpredictable escalation of climate change in less than a decade. Any response, physical or institutional, will take at least that long to realize. Sooner rather than later, act we must.

If we are attentive, it may take but one or two devastating droughts and floods bearing biblical comparison to persuade us that our old plumbing and practices are insufficient to the new extremes of "normal" weather.

Cringe as we may from adding more dams and pipelines to our already over-engineered continent, we'll still need to find new places to store a little of the flood to drink (and grow and make things with) during the drought that is certain to follow. In the event we may favour a few dams or pipes after all.

Solutions

But if we're honest about it, we'll find ways that are smarter, easier, kinder to the planet and, in the long run, cheaper to ourselves.

Using landscaping rather than dikes to temper extremes of rainfall.

Distributing our next big reservoir virtually among a thousand home cisterns or stashing it invisibly underground.

Piping industrial zones for the commercial exchange of wastewater.

Protecting rivers by preserving (and re-establishing) wetlands that filter their living water.

Even letting our beloved lawns go brown through August.

Solutions to our avoidable water "crisis" are at every hand, within reach of each of us.

They are ready to be unleashed by one critical concession: a more candid accounting of nature's services to our market economy. Our most successful strategy will integrate our human industrial economy back into nature's biological one wherever possible, adopting and sharing the planet's own design for responsive, long-term resilience.

Plainly we can do that most effectively if we respect nature's arena of action, the watershed. We must put differences across arbitrary borders into perspective against the larger stakes that we have in common.

The biggest reason Canada's aqua-nationalists are wrong in their isolationism is finally this: We can only do what we need for ourselves by working, and *acting*, together with the neighbours.

Periodical and Internet Sources Bibliography

The following articles have been selected to supplement the diverse views presented in this chapter.

Becky Akers	"My Country Has Trampled on Its Constitution," *Ottawa Citizen*, August 25, 2010.
David Akin	"Canada Can't Ignore Khadr," *Toronto Sun*, July 17, 2010.
Michael Coren	"Bring Khadr Home," *Toronto Sun*, August 14, 2010.
Irwin Cotler	"Ottawa Should Respect the Charter, and Bring Khadr Home," *Gazette* (Montreal), July 13, 2010.
Christopher Flavelle	"What's the Matter with Canada?" *Slate*, September 12, 2008.
Ezra Levant	"Don't Cry for Khadr," *Toronto Sun*, August 10, 2010.
Stephen Marche	"Neighbors Without Benefits," *New Republic*, January 29, 2009.
Michael Medved	"Question for Conservatives: Is Canada Evil?" Townhall.com, April 7, 2010. http://townhall.com.
Sheila Pratt	"Khadr's Edmonton Lawyers Fight to Force Review on Repatriation," *Edmonton Journal*, June 9, 2010.
Carol Rosenberg	"Khadr Trial Will Be a Window into America's War on Terror," McClatchy Newspapers, August 7, 2010.
Keith Spicer	"Why the Silence on Khadr?" *Ottawa Citizen*, August 14, 2010.

For Further Discussion

Chapter 1

1. Kenneth P. Green and Ben Eisen outline the environmental progress that Canada has made in the past several years. Jonathan Gatehouse points out that some of Canada's environmental policies have stirred up controversy. After reading both viewpoints, what is your perception of how Canada rates environmentally? What have been its biggest successes? What are Canada's biggest challenges?

2. During the recent health care debate in the United States, much attention was paid to Canada's health care system. In her viewpoint, Holly Dressel praises Canada's health care system. Doug Wilson, however, derides it in his viewpoint. Review the opinions of both authors. Which viewpoint best represents your view and why?

3. Is Quebec sovereignty a viable and relevant issue in the twenty-first century? Read viewpoints written by Conrad Black and CK to inform your answer.

Chapter 2

1. Canadian participation in the Afghanistan war has generated enormous controversy in Canada. In Tim Fernholz's viewpoint, he finds Canadian involvement to be invaluable and much needed. David Orchard argues for a quick withdrawal of Canadian troops from the conflict. What are your opinions on the Canadian role in Afghanistan?

2. In recent years, the debate over Arctic sovereignty has heated up, with Canada claiming preeminence over other countries such as Russia and the United States. Review Stephen Harper's speech on the issue and the viewpoint of

Mike Blanchfield and Randy Boswell to learn about both sides of the issue. Should Canada keep pressing its claim on the Arctic?

3. Gerry Barr contends that Canada should not slash foreign aid. Beverley J. Oda argues that the amount of aid is not the issue—using it more efficiently to help more people is. After considering both perspectives, outline your plan for Canadian foreign aid policy using the information you've learned.

Chapter 3

1. Have Canada's human rights commissions gone too far? Or are they necessary to protect free speech? Read viewpoints written by Ezra Levant, Jennifer Lynch, and Aaron Goldstein to inform your opinion.

2. Quebec's proposed ban on the niqab has generated much debate in Canada. Thea Lim outlines her reasons for opposing it. Do you feel that the ban goes too far? Provide evidence for your opinion.

Chapter 4

1. What is the nature of the "special relationship" between Canada and the United States? In the first few viewpoints of this chapter, the US Department of State and Brian Bow attempt to answer that question. After reading both views, elucidate your opinion on this "special relationship" using information found in the viewpoints.

2. The case of Omar Khadr has spurred much debate in both Canada and the United States. Dahlia Lithwick argues that Canada should intervene in the case, while Sheldon Alberts and Steven Edwards underscore the government's reluctance to get involved in US affairs. After reading both viewpoints, weigh in on what you think Canada should do in this controversial case.

3. In his viewpoint, Paul Rosenzweig asserts that Canadian security policies are too lax and have caused tension with the United States. Luiza Ch. Savage and John Geddes counter that view, suggesting that US security policies are too stringent. With which view do you agree? Why?

4. The growing water crisis in parts of America has led to heated tension between Canada and the United States. Tony Clarke contends that Canada should enact policies to protect its water from the United States. Chris Wood believes that there is room for negotiation and that Canada could benefit from sharing its water. After reading both views on the issue, explain your opinion on the water controversy.

Organizations to Contact

The editors have compiled the following list of organizations concerned with the issues debated in this book. The descriptions are derived from materials provided by the organizations. All have publications or information available for interested readers. The list was compiled on the date of publication of the present volume; the information provided here may change. Be aware that many organizations take several weeks or longer to respond to inquiries, so allow as much time as possible.

Canada Council for the Arts

350 Albert Street, PO Box 1047, Ottawa, Ontario   KIP 5V8
   Canada
(613) 566-4414 • fax: (613) 566-4390
website: www.canadacouncil.ca

The Canada Council for the Arts is Canada's national arts funding agency, providing financial grants to artists and arts organizations throughout the country. It administers the Canada Council Art Bank, the Public Lending Right Commission, and the Canadian Commission for UNESCO, which coordinates participation of Canadian organizations in the United Nations Educational, Scientific and Cultural Organization. The Canada Council for the Arts also performs research on the state of art and art funding as well as contemporary trends. The council's website links to transcripts of speeches, fact sheets, and other information on the arts in Canada.

Canadian Association of Petroleum Producers (CAPP)

2100, 350-7 Avenue SW, Calgary, Alberta   T2P 3N9
   Canada
(403) 267-1100 • fax: (403) 261-4622
e-mail: communication@capp.ca
website: www.capp.ca

The Canadian Association of Petroleum Producers (CAPP) is an association of Canadian companies that works to explore and develop oil and natural gas reserves across Canada. CAPP strives to foster improvements in the industry's environment, safety, and health performance while facilitating profits and success in the field. The association has compiled wide-ranging statistical information on the Canadian oil and natural gas industry in its Statistical Handbook, which can be found on the website. CAPP also publishes oil forecasts, comprehensive industry reports, and in-depth studies of relevant issues pertinent to petroleum production.

Canadian Human Rights Commission (CHRC)

334 Slater Street, 8th Floor, Ottawa, Ontario   K1A 1E1
(613) 995-1151 • fax: (613) 996-9661
website: www.chrc-ccdp.gc.ca

The Canadian Human Rights Commission (CHRC) investigates and mediates workplace discrimination complaints and develops programs to end discrimination. It also ensures that there are "equal opportunities for employment to the four designated groups: women, Aboriginal peoples, persons with disabilities, and members of visible minorities." The CHRC website has links to its full library of publications, DVDs, posters, and promotional and educational materials. The CHRC publishes a range of reports, such as the recent *Freedom of Expression and Freedom from Hate in the Internet Age.*

Canadian Race Relations Foundation (CRRF)

4576 Yonge, Suite 701, Toronto, Ontario   M2N 6N4
  Canada
(416) 952-3500 • fax: (416) 952-3326
website: www.crr.ca

Established in 1996, the Canadian Race Relations Foundation (CRRF) is "Canada's leading agency dedicated to the elimination of racism in the country." The CRRF works with government agencies, nongovernmental organizations (NGOs), and the national and international community to develop programs and policies to address systematic and institutional racism. The CRRF's Education and Training Centre (ETCentre) develops and coordinates workshops and other educational and training programs focused on addressing and alleviating racism and bigotry. On the CRRF website, individuals can find links to briefs, position papers, fact sheets, and in-depth reports on relevant topics as well as updated information on recent programs and initiatives.

Canadian Tourism Commission (CTC)
Suite 1400, Four Bentall Centre
1055 Dunsmuir Street, Box 49230
Vancouver, British Columbia V7X 1L2
   Canada
(604) 638-8300
website: http://en-corporate.canada.travel

The Canadian Tourism Commission (CTC) promotes tourism in Canada by working in partnership with the Canadian government, private businesses, and the international travel industry. The CTC develops sales and marketing campaigns to increase Canada's share of the international travel market; promotes domestic tourism; and disseminates research and information on Canada's tourism industry. It publishes the *CTC News*, a newsletter that informs readers about the latest research, marketing programs, industry news, and tourism trends. The CTC also provides video and photo galleries of Canadian tourist destinations and must-see attractions.

Environment Canada (EC)
351 St. Joseph Boulevard, Place Vincent Massey, 8th Floor
Gatineau, Quebec K1A 0H3
   Canada
(819) 997-2800 • fax: (819) 994-1412
e-mail: enviroinfo@ec.gc.ca
website: www.ec.gc.ca

Environment Canada (EC) is a Canadian government agency that strives to protect Canada's environment and provides accurate weather and environmental predictions. EC's programs educate Canadians as to how to conserve their natural heritage and protect their surroundings. It also coordinates the federal government's environmental policies and programs, conducts inspections, and initiates prosecutions of polluters and violators. EC publishes more than seven hundred peer-reviewed scientific publications; on its website individuals can peruse the publications available.

Equitas—International Centre for Human Rights Education
666 Sherbrooke West, Suite 1100
Montreal, Quebec   H3A 1E7
  Canada
(514) 954-0382 • fax: (514) 954-0659
e-mail: info@equitas.org
website: www.equitas.org

Established in 1967, Equitas is a nonprofit, nongovernmental organization that creates educational programs to advance democracy, human development, and social justice. As described on its website, "Equitas' capacity-building programs in Canada and abroad have assisted civil society organizations and government institutions to participate effectively in human rights debates, to challenge discriminatory attitudes and practices and to advance important policy and legislative reforms to enhance human rights protection and fulfillment." The organization publishes a newsletter, the *Equitas News*, which explores human rights issues in an in-depth manner and provides updates and information on relevant topics.

Foreign Affairs and International Trade Canada
125 Sussex Drive, Ottawa, Ontario   K1A 0G2
  Canada
(613) 944-4000 • fax: (613) 996-9709
e-mail: engserv@international.gc.ca
website: www.international.gc.ca

Foreign Affairs and International Trade Canada is tasked with strengthening and improving trade agreements and expanding free and fair market access at bilateral, regional, and global levels. It works with government agencies and private businesses to broaden economic opportunities and achievements and to provide a level of economic security for Canada's economy. It is also responsible for coordinating international educational programs and international scholarships for Canadian students interested in studying abroad or international students interested in studying in Canada. The Foreign Affairs and International Trade Canada website offers updated information on the agency's initiatives and activities, linking to speeches and articles written by department officials on topics of Canadian and worldwide interest.

Health Canada

Address Locator 0900C2, Ottawa, Ontario   K1A 0K9
  Canada
(613) 957-2991 • fax: (613) 941-5366
e-mail: info@hc-sc.gc.ca
website: www.hc-sc.gc.ca

Health Canada is the Canadian government agency that is responsible for health policy and programs designed to improve the health of all Canadians. One of its main tasks is to modernize and improve the Canadian health system. It also monitors health and safety risks, such as disease outbreaks or faulty chemical products, and disseminates information to consumers and the media on current health problems. With the Public Health Agency of Canada, it publishes *It's Your Health*, a newsletter that explores a wide range of health and nutritional issues. The Health Canada website provides the most up-to-date warnings, risk assessments, and articles on health issues relevant to Canadian citizens.

Industry Canada (IC)

235 Queen Street, C.D. Howe Building, Ottawa
Ontario   K1A 0H5
  Canada
(613) 954-5031 • fax: (613) 954-2340
e-mail: info@ic.gc.ca

website: www.ic.gc.ca

Industry Canada (IC) is a Canadian government agency that is responsible for developing programs and policies that foster a healthy, balanced, competitive, Canadian economy. According to the agency's website, programs initiated by IC "include developing industry and technology capability, fostering scientific research, setting telecommunications policy, promoting investment and trade, promoting tourism and small business development, and setting rules and services that support the effective operation of the marketplace." Industry Canada publishes a range of newsletters in different subject areas that are available on its website. One of them, *IC Monthly Headlines*, is a general interest publication that provides links to the latest articles, documents, products, and research performed by IC.

Natural Resources Canada (NRCan)
580 Booth, Ottawa, Ontario   K1A 0E4
   Canada
(613) 995-0947
website: www.nrcan.gc.ca

Natural Resources Canada (NRCan) is a government department that fights for the responsible development and use of Canada's natural resources. It conducts advanced research and develops technologies that enable Canada to be a leader in the natural resources sector. NRCan also represents Canada at the international level to negotiate global agreements on the sustainable development of natural resources and the safest, most efficient utilization of such resources. It publishes a range of studies and reports in several topic areas—forests, minerals and mining, energy, and climate change—which are available on the its website. The site also has links to NRCan's three newsletters: *Natural Elements, Heads Up Energy Efficiency*, and *Heads Up CIPEC (Canadian Industry Program for Energy Conservation)*.

Public Safety Canada
269 Laurier Avenue West, Ottawa, Ontario   K1A 0P8
   Canada

(613) 944-4875 • fax: (613) 954-5186
e-mail: communications@ps.gc.ca
website: www.publicsafety.gc.ca

Public Safety Canada is the federal agency responsible for protecting Canadians from natural disasters, crime, and terrorism by coordinating the national security efforts of federal and local organizations, first responders, community groups, and businesses. It runs the Government Operations Centre, which monitors potential threats to national security and implements policies that protect the national interest. Public Safety Canada develops crime prevention programs and policies. The department publishes a range of publications in such subject areas as emergency management, crime prevention, law enforcement, and corrections.

Bibliography of Books

Michael Adams   *Fire and Ice: United States, Canada,*
                 and the Myth of Converging Values.
                 Toronto: Penguin Canada, 2003.

Pat Armstrong   *Wasting Away: The Undermining of*
and Hugh   *Canadian Health Care.* 2nd ed. New
Armstrong   York: Oxford University Press, 2003.

Sylvia Bashevkin, *Opening Doors Wider: Women's*
ed.   *Political Engagement in Canada.*
                   Vancouver: UBC Press, 2009.

Brian Bow   *The Politics of Linkage: Power,*
                 Interdependence and Ideas in
                 Canada-US Relations. Vancouver:
                 UBC Press, 2009.

Brian Bow and   *An Independent Foreign Policy for*
Patrick Lennox, *Canada? Challenges and Choices for*
eds.   *the Future.* Toronto: University of
                 Toronto Press, 2008.

Gerard W.   *National Health Insurance in the*
Boychuk   *United States and Canada: Race,*
                 Territory, and the Roots of Difference.
                 Washington, DC: Georgetown
                 University Press, 2008.

Michael Byers   *Who Owns the Arctic? Understanding*
                 Sovereignty Disputes in the North.
                 Vancouver: Douglas & McIntyre,
                 2009.

Bruno
Charbonneau and
Wayne S. Cox,
eds.

Locating Global Order: American Power and Canadian Security After 9/11. Vancouver: University of British Columbia Press, 2010.

Andrew Cohen

While Canada Slept: How We Lost Our Place in the World. Toronto: McClelland & Stewart, 2003.

John C. Courtney
and David E.
Smith, eds.

The Oxford Handbook of Canadian Politics. New York: Oxford University Press, 2010.

David Dyment

Doing the Continental: A New Canadian-American Relationship. Toronto: Dundurn Press, 2010.

Geoffrey Hale and
Monica Gattinger,
eds.

Borders and Bridges: Canada's Policy Relations in North America. Don Mills, Ontario: Oxford University Press, 2010.

Mel Hurtig

The Truth About Canada: Some Important, Some Astonishing, Some Truly Appalling Things All Canadians Should Know About Our Country. Toronto: McClelland & Stewart, 2009.

Jack Jedwab and
Rodrique Landry,
eds.

Life After Forty: Official Languages Policy in Canada. Montreal: McGill-Queen's University Press, 2010.

Evelyn Kallen

Ethnicity and Human Rights in Canada: A Human Rights Perspective on Ethnicity, Racism, and Systemic Inequality. 3rd ed. New York: Oxford University Press, 2003.

Karim-Aly S. Kassam, ed.
Understanding Terror: Perspectives for Canadians. Calgary: University of Calgary Press, 2010.

Patrick Lennox
At Home and Abroad: The Canada-US Relationship and Canada's Place in the World. Vancouver: UBC Press, 2010.

Ezra Levant
Ethical Oil: The Case for Canada's Oilsands. Toronto: McClelland & Stewart, 2010.

Ezra Levant
Shakedown: How Our Government Is Undermining Democracy in the Name of Human Rights. Toronto: McClelland & Stewart, 2009.

Elizabeth May
Losing Confidence: Power, Politics, and the Crisis in Canadian Democracy. Toronto: McClelland & Stewart, 2009.

Desmond Morton
A Short History of Canada. 6th ed. Toronto: McClelland & Stewart, 2006.

Rex Murphy
Canada and Other Matters of Opinion. Toronto: Doubleday Canada, 2009.

John Ralston Saul
A Fair Country: Telling Truths About Canada. Toronto: Penguin Books Canada, 2008.

Jeffrey Simpson, Mark Jaccard, and Nic Rivers
Hot Air: Meeting Canada's Climate Change Challenge. Toronto: McClelland & Stewart, 2008.

Elinor C. Sloan   *Security and Defence in the Terrorist Era: Canada and the United States Homeland.* 2nd ed. Montreal: McGill-Queen's University Press, 2010.

Garth Stevenson   *Unfulfilled Union: Canadian Federalism and National Unity.* 5th ed. Montreal: McGill-Queen's University Press, 2009.

Ed Struzik   *The Big Thaw: Travels in the Melting North.* Mississauga, Ontario: John Wiley & Sons Canada, 2009.

John Herd Thompson and Stephen J. Randall   *Canada and the United States: Ambivalent Allies.* 4th ed. Athens: University of Georgia Press, 2008.

Index